THE POSSIBILITY
OF ALTRUISM

THE
POSSIBILITY OF
ALTRUISM

BY

THOMAS NAGEL

PRINCETON UNIVERSITY PRESS
PRINCETON, NEW JERSEY

Published by Princeton University Press, Princeton, N.J.
In the U.K.: Princeton University Press, Oxford

ISBN 0-691-02002-7 (paperback edition)
ISBN 0-691-07231-0 (hardcover edition)
LCC 78-4323

FIRST PRINCETON PAPERBACK printing, 1978

Princeton University Press books are printed on
acid-free paper, and meet the guidelines
for permanence and durability
of the Committee on Production Guidelines
for Book Longevity of the Council
on Library Resources

Printed in the United States of America

Originally published 1970 by Clarendon Press, Oxford

9 8 7 6

To
DORIS

PREFACE

I SUBMITTED a thesis on this subject for the B.Phil. at Oxford in 1960, and another for the Ph.D. at Harvard in 1963. Parts of the material were presented to seminars at Berkeley and Princeton, and parts have been seen in mimeograph by friends at other universities. I am grateful to numerous teachers, students, and colleagues for their criticisms and suggestions. My greatest debts are to Gilbert Harman, Robert Nozick, David Wiggins, and especially to John Rawls, who supervised my dissertation at Harvard, and whose influence on my philosophical ideas has been continuous since I was an undergraduate at Cornell.

The first draft of this book was written in 1966-67, when I held a Guggenheim fellowship, and I am deeply grateful to the Guggenheim Foundation for making that period of free time possible.

T.N.

Princeton University
September 1969

POSTSCRIPT

THIS BOOK defends the claim that only objective reasons are acceptable, and that subjective reasons are legitimate only if they can be derived from objective ones. I now think that the argument actually establishes a different conclusion: That there are objective reasons corresponding to all subjective ones. This by itself does not imply that all reasons are objective. It remains possible that the original subjective reasons from which the others are generated retain some independent force and are not completely subsumed under them. What gives rise to a parallel system of objective reasons is the need to avoid motivational dissociation between the personal and impersonal standpoints. But radical dissociation can be avoided without completely subordinating the personal to the impersonal. Unless all degrees of dissociation are excluded, the subjective reasons that provide our starting point may continue to exert a legitimate independent influence in the lives of those who acknowledge parallel objective reasons as well, for the personal standpoint may retain its power after the claims of the impersonal have been acknowledged. The resulting system of reasons, though more complicated, would still explain the possibility of altruism.

March 1978

CONTENTS

PART ONE

ETHICS AND HUMAN MOTIVATION

I

THE FOUNDATION OF MORALS

1. Just as there are rational requirements on thought, there are rational requirements on action, and altruism is one of them. This book defends a conception of ethics, and a related conception of human nature, according to which certain important moral principles state rational conditions on desire and action which derive from a basic requirement of altruism. Altruism itself depends on a recognition of the reality of other persons, and on the equivalent capacity to regard oneself as merely one individual among many.

I conceive ethics as a branch of psychology. My claims concern its foundation, or ultimate motivational basis. If the requirements of ethics are rational requirements, it follows that the motive for submitting to them must be one which it would be contrary to reason to ignore. So it must be shown that susceptibility to certain motivational influences, including altruism, is a condition of rationality, just as the capacity to accept certain theoretical arguments is thought to be a condition of rationality. The view presented here is opposed not only to ethical relativism but to any demand that the claims of ethics appeal to our interests: either self-interest or the interest we may happen to take in other things and other persons. The altruism which in my view underlies ethics is not to be confused with generalized affection for the human race. It is not a feeling.

2. Philosophers interested in the motivational problems of ethics commonly seek a *justification* for being moral: a consideration which can persuade everyone or nearly everyone to adhere to certain moral principles, by connecting those principles with a motivational influence to which everyone is susceptible. The question arises, however, whether any grounding of this sort can meet the conditions of inescapability which should attach to ethics. Any justification, it would seem, must rest on empirical assumptions about the influences to which people are susceptible.

The justification will have neither validity nor persuasive force if those assumptions are not true of the individual to whom it is addressed.

One can escape a rational requirement if one fails to meet its conditions in some way. One is then allowed to beg off, and the permissible grounds depend on the general principle from which the particular application of the requirement follows. That principle may in turn apply in virtue of a still more general principle plus further conditions, and if those conditions are not met, escape is again possible. But at some point the retreat must come to an end: one must reach a requirement (it need not be conditional, for it may have been the original one) from which it is not possible to escape by begging off. It is natural to suppose that principles of this sort must underlie ethics, if it exists.

It is also natural to assume that the enterprise of justification should focus on these basic requirments, thus yielding an ethical system with cast iron motivational backing. But such a programme appears doomed from the start. For if we justify a requirement, it is in terms of a principle from which that requirement follows, perhaps with the aid of further conditions. But that principle must itself represent a requirement, or else what it is adduced to justify will not be one. Therefore any requirement which we set out to justify will not be ultimate. Something beyond justification is required.

3. I assume that a normative requirement on action must have correspondingly strict motivational backing. If ethics is to contain practical requirements, motivation theory, specifically the theory of rational motivation, must contain results that are similarly inescapable. It may be thought that this excludes from an essential role in the foundation of ethics the factor of desire (although it is a mystery how one could account for the motivational source of ethical action without referring to desires). The problem about appealing ultimately to human desires is that this appears to exclude rational criticism of ethical motivations at the most fundamental level. As ordinarily conceived, any desire, even if it is in fact universal, is nevertheless merely an affection (not susceptible to rational assessment) to which one is either subject or not. If that is so, then moral considerations whose persuasiveness depends on desires depend ultimately on

attitudes which we are not required to accept. On the other hand, the picture of human motivational structure as a system of given desires connected in certain ways with action is a very appealing one, and it can seem that any persuasive justification of ethical conduct must find its foothold in such a system.

There are two possible paths out of this dilemma, which are not in the end completely distinct. (a) One may dispute the standard views of motivation and of the role which desires play in it; or (b) one may hold that though all motivation involves desire, some desires are open to rational assessment and need not be regarded simply as given inclinations. I shall propose that the basis of ethics in human motivation is something other than desire; but this factor will itself enable us to criticize certain desires as contrary to practical reason.

4. Denial that justification is the appropriate final defence of ethics suggests the familar view that the question 'Why should I be moral?' is senseless or in principle unanswerable. Strictly the suggestion is correct, but not in a sense which supports intuitionism. I believe that an *explanation* can be discovered for the basic principles of ethics, even though it is not a justification. A satisfactory explanation must account for the motivational force appropriate to requirements on action. Psychology, specifically motivation theory, may therefore be the appropriate field in which to make progress in ethical theory. But this appears to involve radical changes in what is thought possible for psychology. Psychological investigation leading to ethical conclusions may require the reintroduction of metaphysics. One does not ordinarily expect to find in motivation theory any principles which lend themselves to interpretation as normative requirements on action. Motivation theory is automatically regarded as an empirical science; it is assumed that at best we may hope to discover the influences to which men are subject and the patterns into which their behaviour falls—perhaps even certain patterns and influences which are universal. But the suggestion that there must be motivational requirements on which to base ethical requirements (or perhaps that the two are identical) seems to demand *a priori* reasoning in motivation theory—something rather unexpected.

This is the possibility which I propose to explore. Human

motivation possesses features which are susceptible to metaphysical investigation and which carry some kind of necessity
(though this last requires elaborate qualification). The need to
find sufficiently firm psychological ground for ethics has prompted the search for such features, but fortunately there is independent support for their existence.

It will in any case not do to rest the motivational influence of
ethical considerations on fortuitous or escapable inclinations.
 Their hold on us must be deep, and it must be essentially tied to
the ethical principles themselves, and to the conditions of their
truth. The alternative is to abandon the objectivity of ethics.
That is a course which cannot be excluded in advance, but it
should not be taken before serious attempts to rescue the subject have failed.

II

THE TRADITIONAL CONTROVERSY

1. The names 'internalism' and 'externalism' have been used to designate two views of the relation between ethics and motivation.[1] Internalism is the view that the presence of a motivation for acting morally is guaranteed by the truth of ethical propositions themselves. On this view the motivation must be so tied to the truth, or meaning, of ethical statements that when in a particular case someone is (or perhaps merely believes that he is) morally required to do something, it follows that he has a motivation for doing it. Externalism holds, on the other hand, that the necessary motivation is not supplied by ethical principles and judgments themselves, and that an additional psychological sanction is required to motivate our compliance. Externalism is compatible with a variety of views about the motivation for being moral. It is even compatible with the view that such a motivation is always present—so long as its presence is not guaranteed by moral judgments themselves, but by something external to ethics. The present discussion attempts to construct the basis of an internalist position.

Internalists appeal to various types of motivation: self-interest, sympathy, benevolence, even the amorphously general 'approval' or 'pro-attitude'. Even emotivism can be counted as an internalist position of sorts, so the conditions which internalism places on the organization of the motivational factor need not be very rigorous. Internalism's appeal derives from the conviction that one cannot accept or assert sincerely any ethical proposition without accepting at least a prima facie motivation for action in accordance with it. Philosophers who believe that there is no room for rational assessment of the basic springs of motivation will tend to be internalists, but at the cost

---

[1] See W. K. Frankena, 'Obligation and Motivation in Recent Moral Philosophy', in *Essays in Moral Philosophy*, ed. A. I. Melden (Seattle, 1958). Frankena derives the terms from W. D. Falk; see ' "Ought" and Motivation', *Proceedings of the Aristotelian Society* (1947–8).

of abandoning claims to moral objectivity. One way to do this is to build motivational content into the meaning of ethical assertions by turning them into expressions of a special sort of inclination, appropriate only when that inclination is present, and rooted only in the motivations of the speaker. The result is a basically anti-rational ethical theory, having as its foundation a commitment, inclination, feeling, or desire that is simply given (though the superstructure may be characterized by a high degree of rational articulation). Motivational content is thereby tied to the meaning of ethical *utterances*—what the speaker means or expresses—rather than to the truth conditions of those utterances, which are left vague or non-existent.

A stronger position, one which ties the motivation to the cognitive content of ethical claims, requires the postulation of motivational influences which one cannot reject once one becomes aware of them. If such influences can be shown to belong to the content of ethics, then someone who recognizes the truth of an ethical claim will have to accept the corresponding motivation.

2. Mill and Moore appear to be externalists. In Moore's case, the attribution is by elimination, for at least in *Principia Ethica*, he does not consider the motivation for being moral at all. Mill devotes a separate chapter of *Utilitarianism* to what he calls the sanctions for the principle of utility. He regards the question as separate from that of the principle's truth, and the answers he provides are unrelated to his arguments for the principle.

On Moore's stated view it can only be regarded as a mysterious fact that people care whether what they do is right or wrong. I suspect, however, that it is really an unrecognized assumption of internalism that underlies Moore's 'refutation' of naturalism. The evaluative factor which is always left out by any naturalistic description of the object of ethical assessment is in fact the relevant inclination or attitude.[1] But Moore did not realize this, and consequently did not produce an internalist position but an externalist one in which a peculiar non-natural quality served to flesh out the content of ethical claims.

[1] This has been observed by R. M. Hare. Cf. pp. 83–4 of *The Language of Morals* (Oxford, 1952).

Such views are, it seems to me, unacceptable on their surface, for they permit someone who has acknowledged that he should do something and has seen *why* it is the case that he should do it to ask whether he has any reason for doing it. Of course one line of retreat from this unacceptable conclusion is to deny that the evaluative portion or aspect of an ethical assertion has any truth value, and to attach the evaluation instead to the individual's expression of the ethical claim.

But if one wishes to tie the requirement of motivational influence to the truth-conditions of moral claims, with the consequence that if someone recognizes their grounds, he cannot but be affected accordingly, then a stricter motivational connection will be required.

3. One example of such a view is provided by Hobbes, whose ethical system is solidly grounded in motivational energies derived from a universal desire for self-preservation. The ethical system is simply a development of certain consequences of that motive in the conduct of a rational and fully informed individual. Human nature is according to Hobbes subject to other, irrational influences as well, so one will not necessarily do what one ought even when one knows what it is; but given the universality and fundamental nature of the desire to live, a recognition of the grounds for one of Hobbes's ethical imperatives cannot fail to move us to some extent.

Hobbes derives the system of moral requirements from the operation of a motivational factor which can be independently understood, together with certain highly general assumptions about the human condition. The basic motive is taken as given, and only its consequences qualify as ethical conclusions. It is not an ethical principle that all men should want to preserve their own lives; so in that sense motivation theory is at the most fundamental level prior to ethics, which constitutes a development of one branch of it. Claims about what we should do simply *are* on this view claims about what we have a certain sort of motivation for doing; ethical arguments are persuasive because, if someone with the assumed desire understands the argument for an ethical conclusion, he must be aware of those circumstances and interconnections which, according to the argument, would motivate him if he were aware of them.

4. The most influential anti-rational internalist is of course Hume. The motivational basis of his ethical system is weaker and less clearly defined than that of Hobbes, since sympathy (later general benevolence), the specifically moral motivation, requires buttressing by self-interest if it is to be sufficiently powerful to resist contrary claims stemming from self-interest directly. But he does make explicit an extremely attractive theory of the justification of action which has had enormous effect on ethical theory. The view is that any justification must appeal to an inclination in the individual to whom it is offered, and that the justification proceeds by drawing connections between that inclination and other things (notably actions) which are means to its satisfaction. The inclination then becomes transferred to these by association, which is what makes persuasive justification possible. If we cast this view in terms of reasons, it will state that among the conditions for the presence of a reason for action there must always be a desire or inclination capable of motivating one to act accordingly.

Hobbes's system satisfies these conditions on justification. In fact he and Hume approach the task in similar ways: both assume that ethics must represent the domain of the objective, the common, in practical matters—i.e., that which all men equally have reason to promote—and both seek a motivational basis for the possibility of such agreement. Hobbes finds it in men's common interest in certain security conditions, social structures, and conventions necessary for the fulfilment of their desire to survive; Hume finds it in the capacity for sympathetic participation in the happiness and unhappiness of others, or even in the mere thought of the likelihood of their happiness or unhappiness. Both regard ethics as a codification of only part of the motivational apparatus; there remains ample room for practical disagreement among men, and, for Hume at least, given the weakness of sympathy in contrast to self-interest, moral considerations alone are by no means decisive.

On Hume's view one begins with psychology, and ethics is an elaboration of it. The basic psychological factors are not themselves brought to light by ethical investigation (though the need for a foundation for ethics may have led to the search for them). And given Hume's famous restrictions on rational assessment of the passions and of preferences, the possibility of justifying morality is strictly limited. Any justification ends finally with the rationally gratuitous presence of the emotion of sympathy; if that condition were not met, one would simply have no reason to be moral. Now it may in fact follow from Hume's theory of imagination that susceptibility to sympathy is a necessary trait of all beings who can think about the feelings of others.[1] But he does not appear to recognize that his psychological factor has this status; so far as he is concerned the edifice of ethics rests on a psychological contingency. In the case of Hobbes, the love of life may be thought somewhat closer to being a necessary motive for human beings. But still the motivational basis is prior to and independent of the ethical system which derives from it. A quite different sort of theory would be necessary to alter that relation of priority.

5. Plato and Aristotle, each in his own way, constitute examples of such a rebellion against the priority of psychology. Both felt, I think, that the motivation for being moral does not come from elsewhere, i.e. from any independently comprehensible desire or feeling. The ethical motivation, even at its most basic level, can on this view be understood only through ethics. But since the issue is not clearly posed by either of these writers, a discussion of their views would require heavier exegetical work than I wish to undertake here.

Fortunately we have a far better example in the person of Kant, who is explicitly and consciously driven by the demand for an ethical system whose motivational grip is not dependent on desires which must simply be taken for granted. His insistence that the imperatives of morality be categorical is essentially an insistence that their application not depend on the presence of a motivational factor prior to ethics, from which they are extracted as consequences. From Kant's efforts one sees what a struggle is required to undercut the priority of ethically neutral motivations, and to put ethical principles themselves at the absolute source of our moral conduct. It seems possible that Kant's postulation of moral interest as the motivating impulse for phenomenal moral behaviour compromised the effort. But

[1] Because he holds that to imagine the feeling or sensation of another is to have a faint copy of that feeling oneself; hence the imagination of the pain of others will itself be painful.

that need not be settled here. We must try to understand Kant's enterprise.

A hypothetical imperative is the only kind which Hume regards as possible. It states what a given desire provides one with a motivation to do, and it applies only if one is subject to that desire. The desire itself is not commanded by the imperative. Consequently no hypothetical imperative can state an unconditional requirement on action.

Kant's effort to produce a categorical imperative is an attempt to discover requirements on action which apply to a man on no conditions about what he wants, how he feels, etc. They must nevertheless be requirements whose validity involves the capacity to be motivated in accordance with them. Since that motivational factor cannot come from a presupposed motivation which is made a condition of the requirements, it must, if it is to exist at all, come from the requirements themselves. That is, what makes the requirements valid for us must itself determine the capacity of our motivational structure to yield corresponding action. Thus, according to Kant, ethics, rather than appropriating an antecedently comprehensible motivational foundation on which to build its requirements, actually uncovers a motivational structure which is specifically ethical and which is explained by precisely what explains those requirements. It is the conception of ourselves as free which he alleges to be the source of our acceptance of the imperatives of morality, and it is the acceptance of the imperatives thus grounded by which he explains moral motivation. This is moreover not a motivational explanation, since instead of making use of the motivational system, it explains one of its fundamental features.

III

THE SOLUTION

1. The issue of priority between ethics and motivation theory is for an internalist of crucial importance. The position which I shall defend resembles that of Kant in two respects: First, it provides an account of ethical motivation which does not rely on the assumption that a motivational factor is already present among the *conditions* of any moral requirement. On this view the possibility of appropriate motivation must be guaranteed by the truth of the moral claim itself—but *not* because the existence of such motivation is included in advance among the independently comprehensible truth conditions of every moral claim. There are reasons for action which are specifically moral; it is because they represent moral requirements that they can motivate, and not vice versa.

If this is correct, ethics must yield discoveries about human motivation. But of what kind? Not just information about what people want. If ethics is not to presuppose any motivations, but must instead reveal their possibility, the discoveries must be at a more fundamental level than that.

Admittedly other internalist theories, of the Humian sort, offer to explain how the motivation of ethical conduct is possible. Hobbes's theory begins with a desire for self-preservation, and requirements of contractual fidelity and political allegiance are deduced therefrom by a complicated argument which shows how the postulated interest can motivate one to adhere to those requirements. Such a derivation does not start from scratch, however; the basic motivation is presupposed even though ethics reveals the possibility of its extended influence (thereby extending its *actual* influence). Ethical theory does not, in the system of Hobbes, explain how the fear of death is possible. So there is a component in human motivation, which can be understood independently of ethics, on which the force of ethics ultimately depends. That is the sort of dependence that I contend must be eliminated from ethical theory.

Certain ethical principles are themselves propositions of motivation theory so fundamental that they cannot be derived from or defined in terms of previously understood motivations. These principles specify how reasons for action follow from certain given conditions. Thus they *define* motivational possibilities, rather than presupposing them. Consequently the final understanding of action motivated by those reasons will be ethical. To understand the motivation we must understand how the ethical principle governs us.

The second way in which my position resembles Kant's is that it assigns a central role in the operation of ethical motives to a certain feature of the agent's metaphysical conception of himself. On Kant's view the conception is that of freedom, whereas on my view it is the conception of oneself as merely a person among others equally real. However, different as they are, both are thought to be conceptions which we cannot escape, and are thought to provide that basis for ethical motivation which in other internalist theories is provided by various motives and desires. Because of the alleged inescapability of these conceptions, a view of the Kantian type entails that we are not fully free to be amoral, or insusceptible to moral claims. That is what makes us men.

2. I shall argue that the motivational counterpart of an ethical requirement is not any particular desire or sentiment, but rather a matter of structure. Any theory of motivation must contain some structural features. They may be very simple. In the limiting case, they may amount simply to the conditions on causal explanation in general, without special features facilitating its application to human conduct. Even the simplest drive theory assumes some additional structure; a theory which explains all rational action by the combination of desires and beliefs assumes somewhat more. I suggest that the contribution of structural factors to the generation of reasons, and of actions done for those reasons, is very important. That is where the foundation of ethics must be sought (though by no means all of the important structural contributions will be ethical).

We are therefore in search of principles which belong both to ethics and to motivation theory, and which state structural conditions on the forms and interrelations of reasons for action. This solution may appear to involve an illegitimate conflation

of explanatory and normative inquiries. But a close connection
between the two is already embodied in the ordinary concept
of a reason, for we can adduce reasons either to explain or to
justify action. We may explain what a man does by referring to
his reasons. On the other hand we may assert that circumstances
provide someone with a reason to act in certain ways, without
implying that he will be accordingly motivated (if only because
of the possibility of his ignorance). But though the explanatory
and normative claims can diverge, this does not mean that we
are faced with two disparate concepts finding refuge in a single
word. When action is explained by reasons, it is brought under
the control of normative principles. A consideration can operate
as a motivating reason only if it has, or is thought to have, the
status of a reason in the system of normative principles by which
individuals govern their conduct. Such normative principles
therefore specify significant features of the motivational structure. This structure is neither arbitrary nor accidental. Its
form is determined in certain ways by the fact that conscious
beings must apply the system of normative principles to themselves when forming their intentions.

3. The eventual goal of our investigation is an analysis of
altruism along the above lines. However, such an analysis can
emerge only as the result of a broader examination of reasons,
which will include detailed attention to the motive of prudence
as well. Actually, the notions of prudence and altruism indicate
a range of motives narrower than that to be discussed; the conclusions which I shall defend are quite general. My aim is to discover for prudence and altruism, and other motivations related
to them, a basis which depends not on desires, but rather on
formal aspects of practical reason. One of the steps in the
argument will be to show that the most natural alternative,
namely explanation by means of desires, cannot adequately
account for the facts, so that another account is necessary. The
detailed support for this general thesis will be presented in connection with prudence: a less controversial motive, which provides the model for a subsequent analysis of altruism.

The general thesis to be defended concerning altruism is that
one has a *direct* reason to promote the interests of others—a
reason which does not depend on intermediate factors such as

one's own interests or one's antecedent sentiments of sympathy and benevolence. This is both a claim of ethics, and a claim about what happens when someone is altruistically motivated. In this general form it cannot of course yield detailed ethical consequences, and it should not be assumed in advance that the resulting system will be act-utilitarianism, rule-utilitarianism, or any of the other specific alternatives. That can emerge only from a more precise specification of the direct altruistic reasons, which will be determined by the argument. The resulting system will also depend heavily on the analysis of reasons stemming from self-interest, and on their interrelations. Altruistic reasons are parasitic upon self-interested ones; the circumstances in the lives of others which altruism requires us to consider are circumstances which those others already have reason to consider from a self-interested point of view. Therefore the form of altruistic reasons will depend both on the form of self-interested ones, and on the procedure for constructing the altruistic analogue of a given self-interested reason.[1]

The discussion of prudential reasons precedes the defence of altruism and serves as a prototype for it. I shall argue that our own future interests provide us, by themselves, with reasons for present action to secure them, and that motivation of this sort cannot and need not be explained by intermediate present desires, or any other intermediate motive.[2] Since the two claims

[1] It must be emphasized that by altruism I do not mean only the variety of noble self-sacrifice often associated with that epithet. I mean any behaviour motivated merely by the belief that someone else will benefit or avoid harm by it. Our lives are filled with such behaviour; most of it is mundane considerateness which costs us nothing, and involves neither self-sacrifice nor nobility—as when we tell someone he has a flat tyre, or a wasp on his hamburger. Because of its connotations, the word 'altruism' seems inappropriate in such cases, but since there is no more general term to cover them all, I shall use 'altruism' henceforth without further apology. As will be seen, similar qualifications attach to my use of the word 'prudence'.

[2] The importance of this issue, and its close connection with the dispute between egoism and altruism, was stressed by Sidgwick:

> I do not see why the axiom of Prudence should not be questioned, when it conflicts with present inclination, on a ground similar to that on which Egoists refuse to admit the axiom of Rational Benevolence. If the Utilitarian has to answer the question, 'Why should I sacrifice my own happiness for the greater happiness of another?' it must surely be admissible to ask the Egoist, 'Why should I sacrifice a present pleasure for a greater one in the future? Why should I concern myself about my own future feelings any more than about the feelings of other persons?' (*The Methods of Ethics*, 5th edn., London, 1893, p. 418.)

are obviously parallel, a defence of the less controversial motive of prudence may help us to defend the rationality of altruism; but it is relevant also in so far as it elucidates the concept of self-interest, which altruism must always, as it were, take as its argument. Only if we know what people have reason to do for themselves can we discover what, if anything, others have reason to do for them.

IV

NECESSITY AND INTERPRETATION

1. The method which I propose to adopt for the explanation and defence of the stated conditions on rational action, is a method of *interpretation*. It can be adequately conveyed only by examples, and these form the substance of the argument. Nevertheless some remarks of a negative character may be made about it in advance.

The interpretation of a principle will not be a motivational explanation of our adherence to that principle. Since the principles being explained themselves specify the basic framework for certain types of motivational explanation, they will not in turn be capable of motivational explanation, since that would require a framework still more basic, which would mean the original principles were not ultimate after all.

For similar reasons interpretation is not a species of justification. A justification must proceed within the context of a system of reasons, by showing that certain conditions are met which provide sufficient reason for that which is being justified. Since my claims concern the formal character of any system of reasons (whether conceived as explanatory or as normative) which can provide the context for particular rational justifications, there can be nothing more fundamental to appeal to in the way of *reasons* for adhering to the specified conditions. They lie beyond the range of justification.

 Interpretation is an attempt to link these practical principles to equally basic features of the conception which each person has of himself and of his relation to the world, and to link the two in such a way that adherence to the principles can be seen as a practical expression of the conception. The method is that of metaphysical ethics: moral and other practical requirements are grounded in a metaphysics of action, and finally in a metaphysics of the person. The more central and unavoidable is the conception of oneself on which the possibility of moral motivation can be shown to depend, the closer we will have come to demonstrating that the demands of ethics are inescapable.

At this point it is possible only to indicate in a general way the interpretations that will be offered of prudence and altruism. Just as there are formal parallels between prudence and altruism, so there will be parallels between their interpretations. The principle of prudence is connected with a conception of one's present situation as merely a stage in a temporally extended life. It arises from the human capacity to view the present simultaneously as 'now' and as a particular time, tenselessly specifiable. The principle of altruism, on the other hand, is connected with the conception of oneself as merely one person among others. It arises from the capacity to view oneself simultaneously as 'I' and as *someone*—an impersonally specifiable individual.

So we have two conceptions, each with two aspects. It is the necessity of retaining both aspects of each conception, and of avoiding radical conflict between the members of each pair, that gives rise to the two interpretations. That is, if one is to retain the dual conception of oneself as 'I' and as 'someone', without having it come apart in practical reasoning, one must accept certain formal conditions on reasons, which imply a requirement of altruism. Prudence is correspondingly related to the dual conception of the present as 'now' and 'sometime'. To say more at this point would be premature.

2. There is one further negative point to be made, and it is this: My emphasis on the inescapability of ethical requirements and my description of the investigation as *a priori* psychology or metaphysical ethics should not be taken to imply that I propose to discover necessary truths about how human beings actually operate. The topics of necessity, contingency, and possibility are dangerous ones, and I should prefer to avoid any pronouncements about the modal status of my claims. I have no confidence that it is a necessary truth that we are constituted as we are, in the fundamental respects which give rise to our susceptibility to moral considerations. But if we were not so constituted, we should be unrecognizably different, and that may be enough for the purpose of the argument.

There is to be sure a trivial sense in which necessity may be

said to attach to the requirements of practical reason: namely,
that a being who is perfectly rational will necessarily adhere to
them (including those of ethics if there are any). But this is useless as an account of the necessity of ethics, since rationality can
be defined only in terms of adherence to rational requirements.
One cannot discover or justify the principles which specify those
requirements by deriving them from the concept of rationality,
since it is precisely those requirements which define the concept,
and they must be rendered plausible as requirements
independently.

3. There are parallels here to the case of requirements on
theoretical reason. This is a large topic in its own right, and
cannot be adequately treated here.[1] Nevertheless a few observations are in order. Theoretical requirements say what we
must think, what we *must* conclude from given premises, but it is
not clear in precisely what sense they say this. To what extent
can logic be regarded as a branch of psychology? Requirements of theoretical reason do not appear to state how we
necessarily do think, nor how we necessarily would think under
some condition or other. The suggestion that they state how a
perfectly rational being necessarily would think has the same
emptiness that its analogue has in the practical case.

What we find in both cases are certain patterns of thought
and reasoning whose appeal for us is inescapable—patterns by
which we correct ourselves when we stray, and in terms of which
we acknowledge criticism from others. This is what makes it
plausible to regard logic as a normative science. What we find
in neither case, on the other hand, is the possibility of analysing
rational requirement in terms of entailment. That is, the acceptance of certain conclusions is not entailed by the acceptance of
certain premises, even if those conclusions themselves are entailed by those premises.[2]

In fact acceptance of the conclusion does not appear to be
entailed even if one supplements belief of the premises with the
belief *that* the premises entail the conclusion. The same can be

[1] The similarities between practical and theoretical reasoning have been usefully
explored by R. Edgley. See 'Practical Reason', *Mind* (April, 1965).
[2] The only exception is the degenerate case in which premises and conclusion
are identical.

said of non-deductive theoretical inference; it is logically possible to believe premises which provide non-deductive support
for a conclusion—even to believe *that* they support the conclusion
—without believing the conclusion itself (or even that it is
probable). And in the practical case: acknowledgment of the
conditions which provide reasons for an action, even when combined with the knowledge that they do provide such reasons,
does not entail that one will perform or even want to perform
the act.

We may be tempted to postulate a further logical or inductive
belief which justifies the transition from premises to conclusion
by making the mental connection airtight. The counterpart of
this in the sphere of practical reason is the temptation to postulate an appropriate intermediate desire between reasons and
action: one which simultaneously validates the reasons and
guarantees their motivational efficacy. But in both cases the
addition will fail to accomplish its purpose. To get from the new,
enlarged set of premises to the conclusion still requires a framework of some kind; there must be principles by which the
premises combine to yield justified conclusions, or principles by
which beliefs and desires combine to yield justified actions. One
cannot dispense with this need simply by adding to the premises.

The major disanalogy between theoretical and practical
reasoning, of course, is that the premises of a deductive argument entail its conclusion, even though belief of the one does not
entail belief of the other. Nothing like this is true in the practical case. One might try to construct artificially a propositional
content for the conclusion of a practical syllogism (whose true
conclusion, as Aristotle points out, is an act or intention)—some
claim about sufficient reasons, or simply a conclusion that
something should be done. But even if one were able to pack
the premises in such a way as to make it plausible that this proposition was entailed by them, the whole apparatus would
clearly be parasitic on the original requirement of practical
reason, which involved no entailment, but only a requirement
of a different kind. It is instructive that a similar position can be
taken in regard to non-deductive inference. Claims to the effect
that certain premises confirm a certain conclusion may be
parasitic on requirements of inductive reasoning which are
ultimately normative and psychological.

And it must be added finally that even deductive argument is not safe from this type of construction—i.e. the view that our talk of entailment is really parasitic on psychological necessity, on the fact that we are forced from one belief to another, and that we feel required to alter our beliefs in response to certain types of systematic criticism. I believe that such a view is common to Quine and Wittgenstein. If it is correct, then the apparent disanalogy between requirements on practical and on theoretical reason disappears. But that is another subject.

What can be asserted with some confidence is that in so far as rational requirements, practical or theoretical, represent conditions on belief and action, such necessity as may attach to them is not logical but natural or psychological. It is therefore necessary to inquire how they achieve their hold on us. Perhaps the most we can hope is that such principles should apply to us in virtue of particularly deep features of our make-up, features which we cannot alter. That is what I hope to establish with regard to certain requirements of practical reason, and that will be the function of the procedure of interpretation.

4. Rational principles are canons for the criticism, justification, and self-determination of thought and action. When they govern people's actions, it is because people apply the principles to themselves, taking into consideration their present circumstances and what the principles indicate to be an appropriate outcome. Kant observed that rational motivation is unique among systems of causation because any explanation of action in terms of the theory refers essentially to the application of its principles by individuals to themselves in the determination of their actions. The same might be said for the rational causation of belief. It is as though billiard balls decided where to roll, and at what velocity, after carefully noting the forces and frictions operating upon them, and inferring the appropriate direction from the laws of mechanics. (They would also have to be capable of correcting themselves, or acknowledging the accuracy of a correction, if they made a mistake.)

The normative requirements embodied in the theory of motivation do not merely describe externally observable (or internally *observable*) patterns; they are internalized, they govern the agent's critical faculty, they characterize him as the source of his actions and thoughts. He does not choose them, for choices must issue from him if they are to be his, and this means that they must be the product of determining principles which constitute him as the source of his choice, and which could not be chosen by him because in their absence there would be no *he* to choose.

The less a person's motivational apparatus is like a sieve or funnel for external influences—the more definition it possesses and is able to impose on the action of those influences—the more sense there is in ascribing actions and decisions to the person as their source. The possibility of *interpreting* ethical and other basic normative principles arises because they define what a person is, if he governs his behaviour in the most general terms according to them. To interpret them is to say more perspicuously what such an individual is like, and how his nature is revealed in various features of the rational apparatus.

There is nothing regrettable about finding oneself, in the last analysis, left with something which one cannot choose to accept or reject. What one is left with is probably just oneself, a core without which there could be no choice belonging to the person at all. Some unchosen restrictions on choice are among the conditions of its possibility.

PART TWO

SUBJECTIVE REASONS AND PRUDENCE

V

DESIRES

1. Beginning with relatively uncontroversial cases, we must try to arrive at general conclusions about the sources of reasons and their mode of operation. Eventually we shall deal with prudence as a model for the treatment of altruism: the difficulties which arise in the two cases depend on similar arguments and fallacies. Most important, the interpretation of that feature of reasons on which prudence depends provides a model for the parallel enterprise in the case of altruism.

I shall argue that the superficially plausible method of accounting for all motivations in terms of the agent's desires will not work, and that the truth is considerably less obvious and more significant. It is therefore necessary to begin with an investigation of the role of desires in rational motivation generally, in order to demonstrate that what they can explain is limited, and that even in simple cases they produce action by a mechanism which is not itself explicable in terms of desires.

The attempt to derive all reasons from desires stems from the acknowledgment that reasons must be capable of motivating, together with an assumption which I shall attack—that all motivation has desire at its source. The natural position to be opposed is this: since all motivated action must result from the operation of some motivating factor within the agent, and since belief cannot by itself produce action, it follows that a desire of the agent must always be operative if the action is to be genuinely his. Anything else, any external factor or belief adduced in explanation of the action, must on this view be connected with it through some desire which the agent has at the time, a desire which can take the action or its goal as object. So any apparently prudential or altruistic act must be explained by the connection between its goal—the agent's future interest or the interest of another—and a desire which activates him now. Essentially this view denies the possibility of motivational action at a distance, whether over time or between persons. It bridges any apparent gaps with desires of the agent, which are thought to supply the necessary links to the future and to external situations.

Prudence cannot on this view be explained merely by the perception that something is in one's future interest; there must be a desire to further one's future interests if the perception is to have an effect. What follows about altruism is similar: I cannot be motivated simply by the knowledge that an act of mine will have certain consequences for the interests of others; I must care what happens to them if this knowledge is to be effective. There seems little doubt that most people have the desire that makes prudence possible, though it is sometimes overcome by other, more immediate impulses. Altruistic or benevolent desires on the other hand seem less common. In neither case are we in any sense required to possess the desires in question: consequently we are not required to act on the specified considerations. If one lacks the relevant desire, there is nothing more to be said.

The consequence of this view, for a system of normative reasons, is that the interests of others, or his own future interests, cannot themselves provide a person with reasons for action unless we are prepared to admit also that reasons by themselves, or conditions sufficient for their presence, may provide us with no motivation for action whatever. The separation of normative from motivational discourse has of course been attempted. But if one finds that move implausible, and wishes some guarantee that reasons will provide a motive, then one is left with no alternative, on the motivational premises already laid out, but to include a present desire of the agent, one with appropriate scope, among the conditions for the presence of any reason for action whatever. Therefore another's interest, or my own future interest, can provide me with a reason—a reason capable of motivating—only if a desire for that object is present in me at the time.

The consequences for any other-regarding morality are extreme, for if one wishes to guarantee its universal application, one must make the presence of reasons for altruistic behaviour depend on a desire present in all men. (No wonder self-interest has so often been preferred to altruism as the foundation for justice and the other social virtues.) This view eliminates the possibility of construing ethical principles so based as requirements on action, unless one can somehow show that the appropriate underlying *desires* are required of us.

2. The assumption that a motivating desire underlies every intentional act depends, I believe, on a confusion between two sorts of desires, motivated and unmotivated. It has been pointed out before[1] that many desires, like many beliefs, are arrived at by decision and after deliberation. They need not simply assail us, though there are certain desires that do, like the appetites and in certain cases the emotions. The same is true of beliefs, for often, as when we simply perceive something, we acquire a belief without arriving at it by decision. The desires which simply come to us are unmotivated though they can be explained. Hunger is produced by lack of food, but is not motivated thereby. A desire to shop for groceries, after discovering nothing appetizing in the refrigerator, is on the other hand motivated by hunger. Rational or motivational explanation is just as much in order for that desire as for the action itself.

The claim that a desire underlies every act is true only if desires are taken to include motivated as well as unmotivated desires, and it is true only in the sense that *whatever* may be the motivation for someone's intentional pursuit of a goal, it becomes in virtue of his pursuit *ipso facto* appropriate to ascribe to him a desire for that goal. But if the desire is a motivated one, the explanation of it will be the same as the explanation of his pursuit, and it is by no means obvious that a desire must enter into this further explanation. Although it will no doubt be generally admitted that some desires are motivated, the issue is whether another desire always lies behind the motivated one, or whether sometimes the motivation of the initial desire involves no reference to another, unmotivated desire.

Therefore it may be admitted as trivial that, for example, considerations about my future welfare or about the interests of others cannot motivate me to act without a desire being present at the time of action. That I have the appropriate desire simply *follows* from the fact that these considerations motivate me; if the likelihood that an act will promote my future happiness motivates me to perform it now, then it is appropriate to ascribe

1. For example by Aristotle: *Nicomachean Ethics*, Book III, Chapter 3.

to me a desire for my own future happiness. But nothing follows about the role of the desire as a condition contributing to the motivational efficacy of those considerations. It is a necessary condition of their efficacy to be sure, but only a logically necessary condition. It is not necessary either as a contributing influence, or as a causal condition.

In fact, if the desire is itself motivated, it and the corresponding motivation will presumably be possible for the same reasons. Thus it remains an open question whether an additional, unmotivated desire must always be found among the conditions of motivation by any other factor whatever. If considerations of future happiness can motivate by themselves, then they can explain and render intelligible the desire for future happiness which is ascribable to anyone whom they do motivate. Alternatively, there may be another factor operating in such cases, one which explains both the motivational influence of considerations about the future and the motivated desire which embodies that influence. But if a further, unmotivated desire is always among those further conditions, it has yet to be proved.

If we bring these observations to bear on the question whether desires are always among the necessary conditions of *reasons* for action, it becomes obvious that there is no reason to believe that they are. Often the desires which an agent necessarily experiences in acting will be motivated exactly as the action is. If the act is motivated by reasons stemming from certain external factors, and the desire to perform it is motivated by those same reasons, the desire obviously cannot be among the conditions for the presence of those reasons. This will be true of any motivated desire which is ascribable to someone simply in virtue of his intentional pursuit of a goal. The fact that the presence of a desire is a logically necessary condition (because it is a logical consequence) of a reason's motivating, does not entail that it is a necessary condition of the *presence* of the reason; and if it is motivated by that reason it *cannot* be among the reason's conditions.

3. As I have said earlier, the temptation to postulate a desire at the root of every motivation is similar to the temptation to postulate a belief behind every inference. Now we can see that the reply in both cases is the same: that this is true in the trivial

sense that a desire or belief is always present when reasons motivate or convince—but not that the desire or belief explains the motivation or conclusion, or provides a reason for it. If someone draws conclusions in accordance with a principle of logic such as *modus ponens*, it is appropriate to ascribe to him the belief that the principle is true; but that belief is explained by the *same* thing which explains his inferences in accordance with the principle. The belief that this principle is true is certainly not among the *conditions* for having reasons to draw conclusions in accordance with it. Rather it is the perception of those reasons which explains both the belief and the particular con-clusions drawn.

Beliefs provide the material for theoretical reasoning, but finally there is something besides belief, namely reason, which underlies our inferences from one set of beliefs to another, and explains both the conclusions and those logical beliefs which embody our inferential principles in general propositional form. Correspondingly, desires are among the materials for practical reasoning, but ultimately something besides desire explains how reasons function. This element accounts for many of the connec-tions between reasons (including the reasons which stem from desires) and action. It also explains those general desires which embody our acceptance of the principles of practical reason.

The omnipresence of desires in action is misleading, for it suggests that a desire must form the basis of every motivation. But in fact, when we examine the logical reason why desire must always be present, we see that it may often be motivated by precisely what motivates the action. An alternative basis for that motivation must therefore be discovered. The alternative which I shall defend does not require one to abandon the assumption that reasons must be capable of motivating. It merely points out that they may have this capacity precisely because they are reasons, and not because a motivationally influential factor is among their conditions of application.

An account in terms of the structure of reasons and their relations to their conditions and to each other has the advantage of rendering the motivation of action by those conditions signi-ficantly more intelligible than does the mere postulation of intervening desires. It explains the peculiar intelligibility of prudential motivation, and also, I hope to show, the possibility of altruistic motivation—both without the assistance of intervening desires for future happiness or the welfare of others.

4. To summarize the argument briefly:

Though all motivation implies the presence of desire, the sense in which this is true does not warrant us in concluding that all motivation requires that desire be operative as a motivational *influence*. To that extent it remains open that there can be motivation without any motivating desire.

Some desires are themselves motivated by reasons. Those desires at any rate cannot be among the conditions of the reasons which motivate them. And since there may in principle be motivation without motivating desires, those reasons may be motivationally efficacious even without the presence of any *further* desires among their conditions.

There are two ways in which this might be so; either some other motivating factor besides desire may be present among the conditions for the existence of those reasons; or else their motivational efficacy may derive not from the conditions themselves, but rather from the principle which governs the derivation of reasons from those conditions.

In the latter event, the motivational efficacy of reasons for action would be due only to the system by which they are derived from their conditions. This would be explained by a connection between the structure of a system of reasons and the structure of human motivation. In that sense it would still be true that a reason is necessarily capable of motivating. That is the possibility which I shall pursue.

VI

PRUDENTIAL MOTIVES AND THE PRESENT

1. Structural influences are apparent even when an unmotiva-ted present desire motivates action. It will be useful to consider such a case before dealing with the more complex example of prudence.

If I am thirsty and a soft-drink machine is available, I shall feed it a dime, open the resulting bottle, and drink. In such a case desire, belief, and rudimentary theoretical reasoning evidently combine somehow to produce action. We should ordinarily say, moreover, that the circumstances provide at least prima facie reason for the act. So two questions must be answered: how does the motivation operate; and what provides the conditions for the presence of a reason?

I shall propose a single answer to both questions: Reasons are transmitted across the relation between ends and means, and that is also the commonest and simplest way that motivational influence is transmitted. No further desires are needed to explain this phenomenon, and moreover, attempts to explain it in such terms are bound to fail.

It must be realized that the case does require an explanation. Upon reflection, it can seem mysterious that *thirst* should be capable of motivating someone not just to drink, but to put a dime in a slot. Thirst by itself does not motivate such technical undertakings; an understanding of currency and the protocol of vending machines is essential. But when these factors have been added to the explanation, we still lack an account of how they combine with the thirst to produce action.

I think it is very important to resist the temptation to close this gap by expanding the original desire for drink, or by adding another desire. It is of course true that when one sees that the only way to get a drink is to put a dime in the slot, one then wants to put a dime in the slot. But that is what requires explanation: it is a desire *motivated* by thirst plus certain information. If we simply add it on as a further motive, we shall not do justice to its peculiar appropriateness; for *any arbitrary* desire might be added on in *that* capacity.

For example, it is imaginable that thirst should cause me to want to put a dime in my pencil sharpener, but this would be an obscure compulsion or the product of malicious conditioning, rather than a rational motivation. We should not say that thirst provided me with a *reason* to do such a thing, or even that thirst had motivated me to do it.

A theory of motivation is defective if it renders intelligible behaviour which is not intelligible. If we explain the ordinary case of adopting means to a desired end in terms of an additional desire or an extension of the original one, then we must allow a similar explanation for counter-rational cases.

But the fact is that such devices do not produce adequate motivational explanations of deranged behaviour. And if they do not yield adequate explanations in the peculiar case, there is reason to believe that their analogues are not the basis of intelligibility in the normal case. The analogous hypotheses seem to fill the motivational gap in the normal case only because they are not actually *needed* to make the behaviour intelligible, whereas in the abnormal case, where something more obviously *is* needed, they do not succeed. This leaves us, if we do not wish to be arbitrary, with the task of dividing the intelligible connections from the unintelligible ones and explaining why the former work and the latter do not.

2. The solution is to confer a privileged status on the relation between ends and means. This is easily incorporated into the definition of a reason. We may say that if being thirsty provides a reason to drink, then it also provides a reason for what enables one to drink. That can be regarded as the consequence of a perfectly general property of reasons for action: that they transmit their influence over the relation between ends and means. An exact statement of the thesis would have to include an analysis of that relation (or another better suited to the present purpose) as well as an account of what reasons are. Both of these questions will be treated at greater length eventually, but the position is clear enough in outline: All reasons are in

some respect general, and this is merely part of the specification of how far their generality extends.

If there is a reason to do something on a particular occasion, it must be specifiable in general terms which allow that same reason to be present on different occasions, perhaps as a reason for doing other things. All such general specifications, whatever else may be true of them, will share a certain formal feature. They will never limit the application of the reason to acts of one sort only, but will always include other acts which promote those of the original kind. And in some cases the general specification will simply assign the reason to all acts that promote some end which is not itself an act. Intuitively, this means that when a person accepts a reason for doing something he attaches value to its occurrence, a value which is either intrinsic or instrumental. In either case the relation of means to ends is involved in the evaluative conception: if the value is intrinsic it attaches derivatively to what will promote the likelihood of the act; if instrumental, the act is valuable as a means to something else, and the same value attaches to other means as well.

In the case with which we began, a desire was among the antecedent conditions of a rational motivation, and the problem was to explain how that desire could extend its motivational influence beyond the scope of its immediate, spontaneous manifestations, through connection with certain beliefs. The system which accounts for this case is operative not only for reasons stemming from desires but for all other reasons as well. Hence it cannot be embodied merely in a constraint on the scope of desires—e.g. an insistence that to desire the end is always to desire the means. Any acceptance of a reason for action must conform to the general principle concerning means and ends. The full influence of desires and of other types of motivation is explained by their interaction with the system. Consequently desires cannot account for its operation.

3. What I propose to do now is to examine this system carefully, and to show how it can be extended to accommodate more complex rational motivations: first prudence and eventually altruism. I shall argue that structural accounts like this accommodate the phenomena of human motivation better than the natural alternatives, and that they reveal more about human beings.

In discussing prudence, we shall be concerned with the element of practical foresight, rather than with any special association the notion may have with self-interest. This must be mentioned because in philosophical usage the term 'prudential' has come to mean approximately the same as 'self-interested', losing even its special connection with provision for the future. This has some foundation in ordinary usage, for we often identify the prudent course of action with that which is personally expedient, and oppose it to selfless as well as to risky alternatives. But I believe that in the most general sense we can perfectly well speak of prudence (or its absence) in cases where the interest of the agent is not in question. When parents concern themselves with the welfare of their children, for example, they may be imprudent not only as regards their own future interests, but also in relation to their children's interests. A person's conduct of an organization's affairs, or his management of another person's investments, may be assessed in the same way. Whatever the case, it is the weight accorded to future consequences which is essential; one is judged imprudent if one disregards them or allows them to be outweighed by insufficient present considerations.

To explain prudential motives, I shall argue that the means-end relation enters into the generation of reasons in such a way as to extend the influence not only of reasons which are present, but also of reasons which are expected in the future. It is therefore a *formal* feature of the system that there is reason to do not only what will promote that for which there is presently a reason, but also what will promote something future for which it is expected that there *will* be a reason. This is, moreover, a perfectly general condition, applying to all reasons, and not just those which stem from desires or interests.

My strategy will be to argue against the most plausible alternative account of prudence; one according to which prudential reasons stem from a present desire for the satisfaction of future interests and desires (or for the long-term satisfaction of all interests, present and future). I shall argue against two assumptions on which this view depends. First, the assumption that a desire or other relevant condition can provide a reason only when it is present. Second, the assumption that any desire with a future object provides a reason for pursuing that object.

After these assumptions have been criticized, I shall present what I take to be the correct account, involving a formal normative structure whose operation does not have to be explained in terms of desires—which itself explains how the influence of desires is extended through a rational system.

An exact determination of the requirements of prudence is not my object. We shall not be concerned to discover how much advance planning is desirable, or to what extent one should live in the present, but rather with the issue how *any* motivation by future considerations is possible. Moreover, having said that prudence need not be self-interest, I shall nevertheless proceed to conduct the discussion primarily in terms of a self-interested case, concentrating on the restricted class of reasons which depend on one's desires and the concern for their future satisfaction. This is partly for simplicity, and partly because that case has features which render alternatives to my position particularly plausible. If I can defend the position there, it will extend relatively easily to other sorts of reasons. The problem is how any considerations about the future, about the long-range outcomes of alternative courses of action, can affect an individual's behaviour in the present.

4. The issue is not whether prudence exists, but over its analysis: the analysis both of prudential motivation and of the conditions for the presence of prudential reasons. It is obvious that people are prudentially motivated and do care what will happen to them; someone who remained totally unmoved by the possibility of avertable future harm or accessible future benefits would be regarded as wildly peculiar by anyone, no matter what his theory of motivation. The issue, by now a familiar one, is whether the effect on present action of beliefs about my future interests must be explained by an intervening desire, or whether the connection can be made through a requirement of practical reason by which actions are governed. If there is such a requirement, codifiable as a condition on reasons, then its operation would take the place of desire in explaining certain motivational connections, connections which indeed could not be explained by a desire.

Against the neutral view that a covering prudential desire is operative, I contend first that it does not take care of the actual cases (i.e. what we can explain in terms of prudence and the actual prudential reasons which we believe to obtain); second, that the cases it does accommodate are not handled in the right way, so that their motivational nature is obscured by the theory; third, that my suggestion sheds more light on the operation of prudence and on human nature in general.

I have already inveighed against the position that a desire must always be present as the source of action and correlatively as a condition for the presence of reasons for action. The same difficulties apply in the present case, where some such conviction is certainly operative. One basis for the view that knowledge of my future desires cannot motivate me to act now without the *help* of a current motivating desire for future satisfaction is that in a trivial sense such knowledge cannot motivate me without a desire being *present*. But that is not because the desire's motivational force is necessary to enable the information to work, but rather because such a desire is ascribable to me *in virtue of* the operation of the motive. Once we have undercut that argument for the omnipresence of desires, we have no reason to believe that a desire must be present as the condition of every reason, in order to guarantee that the reason will, when present, be capable of motivating.

The same applies to the specific case of prudence, and to the insistence that a prudential desire must be present as the condition of both prudential motivation and prudential reasons. That may be true (in the familiar, trivial sense) of prudential *motivation*, but nothing in any case follows for prudential reasons.

One does not of course refute a position by showing that bad arguments may be offered in its support. Fortunately more direct criticisms are available. The hypothesis that all links to the future are made by present desires suggests that the agent at any specific time is insular, that he reaches outside himself to take an interest in his future as one may take an interest in the affairs of a distant country. The relation of a person to temporally distant stages of his life must be closer than that. His concern about his own future does not require an antecedent desire or interest to explain it. There must already be a connection which renders the interest intelligible, and which depends not on his present condition but on the future's being a part of his *life*. A life is not a momentary episode, nor a series of such episodes. I shall now elaborate on these criticisms.

5. The position I am attacking explains prudential conduct by saying that my future interests give me reasons to act because I have a present desire to further those interests. On this view future desires cannot by themselves provide reasons, but present desires can. I wish to begin by criticizing the normative system which embodies this contrast. Granted, on the view under discussion, there is usually in fact present a desire for the satisfaction of future desires, which allows the latter to give rise to reasons at one remove. But it is not unreasonable to examine the general system without reference to the particular prudential desire which it is designed to accommodate, for that after all is not part of the system but a motivational factor which allegedly operates through it. The system is supposed to define how reasons proceed from *any* desire, whether its object be present or future. It is therefore presumably meant to apply to situations in which the prudential desire is absent and other desires with future objects are present—(whether or not such cases actually exist). Consequently we may begin by considering the rational system itself, without assuming the prudential desire.

The two features of the system to which I object are (a) that it does not allow the expectation of a future reason to provide by itself any reason for present action, and (b) that it does allow the present desire for a future object to provide by itself a reason for present action in pursuit of that object. All of the following constitute possibilities under the proposed system:

First, given that any desire with a future object provides a basis for reasons to do what will promote that object, it may happen that I now desire for the future something which I shall not and do not expect to desire then, and which I believe there will then be no reason to bring about. Consequently I may have reason now to prepare to do what I know I will have no reason to do when the time comes.[1]

---

[1] There is one way in which an irrational desire like this might provide legitimate reasons for action: namely, as a source of anxiety troublesome enough to be worth appeasing. Thus if on Saturday I conceive for no reason a strong desire to eat a persimmon on Sunday, although I know I shall not want it on Sunday and shall

Second, suppose that I expect to be assailed by a desire in the future; then I must acknowledge that in the future I will have prima facie reason to do what the desire indicates. But this reason does not obtain now, and cannot by itself apply derivatively to any presently available means to the satisfaction of the future desire. Thus in the absence of any further relevant desire in the present, I may have no reason to prepare for what I know I shall have reason to do tomorrow.

Third, expected future desires whose objects conflict with those of my present desires for the future do not in themselves provide any present countervailing reasons at all—not even prima facie reasons which may be outweighed. Any desires or reasons which are merely expected are motivationally irrelevant. I may now, therefore, have an unopposed reason to promote something future which I will, when it happens, have an unopposed reason to prevent—and if I know what my future desires will be, I may have reason now to do precisely what will ensure the failure of my future *rational* attempts; I may have reason to do what I know I will later have reason to try to undo, and will therefore have to be especially careful to lay traps and insurmountable obstacles in the way of my future self.[1]

A system with consequences such as this not only fails to require the most elementary consistency in conduct over time, but in fact sharpens the possibilities of conflict by grounding an individual's plottings against his future self in the apparatus of rationality. These are formal and extremely general difficulties about the system, since they concern the relation of what is

have no other reason to eat it then (perhaps the same thing happens to me every weekend), I may have *some* reason to buy a persimmon on Saturday (assuming they cannot be purchased on Sunday) simply to preserve my peace of mind on *Saturday*. Note, however, that in this case the desire does not directly provide a reason for pursuit of its object; rather it creates an anxiety which there is reason to dissipate, and which it may be impossible to dissipate except by ensuring the availability of the future object of the desire.

[1] This must not be confused with the perfectly unobjectionable and not uncommon case in which someone puts obstacles in his way knowing that he will *want* something in the future which he should not have. This may induce him to put a time lock on the liquor cabinet, for example. But that is because he expects to want to do what he will *at that time* have reason *not* to do. There is thus a straightforward link in such cases between present and future reasons. One does not have reason now to ensure the frustration of what it will be *rational* to do in the future.

rational to what will be rational, no matter what source of reasons is operative.

6. At the next stage of criticism we reintroduce the prudential desire postulated by proponents of such a system, and see how the system thus supplemented purports to account for the phenomena. But whatever the outcome of this inquiry, the objection of the preceding section remains valid. Addition of the proposed desire cannot dissolve the rational paradox which has been objected to in the theory, because the addition does not set a limit to what the theory allows as rational.[1]

In fact, postulation of a prudential desire does not deal satisfactorily with the problems which I have argued arise in the system without it. First of all, its formulation presents serious problems. Presumably the prudential desire is supposed to yield a result based on the consideration of all other desires (or alternative sources of reasons), past, present, and future. It should obtain the conclusion by striking a balance between claims from different times. However, it is itself simply *one* of the *present* desires, and operates as such. So if one of its objects is the satisfaction of those present desires other than itself, they will enter the calculation of reasons twice: once in their own right, and once as objects of the prudential desire. To avoid this result, the objects of the prudential desire would have to be restricted to *future* satisfaction. But this would not be satisfactory either, for a further balancing mechanism would then be necessary in order to settle conflicts between considerations derived from ordinary present desires and those derived from the future via the prudential desire. Either this mechanism would be a further desire, in which case the same problems would arise all over again—or else it would be a structural feature of the system of

[1] It may be suggested that the dissociated behaviour could be denied to be rational even by this theory, on the ground that the *desires* from which that behaviour derives are so peculiar. But this is to concede my point. For it must mean that while a desire for future satisfaction is rational, certain other desires, namely those for future objects which one knows there will be no reason to pursue in the future, are themselves irrational and confer this irrationality on their behavioural consequences. And the principle which entails the irrationality of those desires will be the same as the one I am defending: namely, that desires for the future *per se* do not ordinarily provide reasons for action, and that action deriving from such desires is rational only when it, and the desires themselves, are justified by reasons expected to hold in the future.

reasons, in which case the project of accounting for prudence in terms of desires would have to be abandoned (as I have maintained).

Secondly, even if this problem could be surmounted, and there *were* a prudential desire, its presence would not alter the fact that the system through which it operates permits the derivation of reasons for action from *any* desire with a future object—not only the prudential one. A desire with a future object does not on this view have to be justified in order to provide reasons for action. Therefore it remains the case, even if the prudential desire is present, that other desires with future objects can provide me with reasons to bring about what I know I shall have no reason to want when the time comes. This will occur if I have a desire for a future object to which I shall in the future be entirely indifferent (and about which the prudential desire is therefore neutral). The system cannot be prevented from generating these unwelcome reasons.

Thirdly, although introduction of a prudential desire may accomplish the primary aim of generating reasons to prepare now for future satisfaction, it at the same time creates new counter-intuitive results. For if it has among its objects the satisfaction of all future desires, this could include the satisfaction of a future desire for a still more future object. So if on Monday I expect that on Tuesday I shall want to eat a persimmon on Wednesday, although I also expect that on Wednesday I shall be indifferent to persimmons (as I am on Monday)—then on Monday I have a clear *prudential* reason to make sure I have a persimmon available on Wednesday, though I will not have any reason to want it then, and I do not on Monday want to have it then.

In other words, the proposed system continues to yield paradoxical results, even after the (unformulable) prudential desire has been added. But finally, even if these problems are set aside, there remains what I regard as the central objection: that even when the proposed view does accommodate the phenomena of rational motivation extensionally, so to speak, it accommodates them in the wrong way, and makes the wrong kind of sense out of them. A person's future should be of interest to him not because it is among his present interests, but because it is *his future.* He already stands in a far stronger and more important relation to his future and the desires he can expect to experience than could possibly be established by any desire which might assail him in the present. The latter sort of connection enables him to reach toward something outside himself; the former depends on an acknowledgment that certain things are not outside to begin with, and that events in his future hold an interest for him now because they belong to a single person of whom his present segment is merely one stage. (This will be elaborated subsequently, and, I hope, rendered less metaphorical.)

7. The above point is reinforced by our final criticism of the view under attack: we must raise the question whether desires with future objects ever give rise to important reasons at all. I have claimed that a prudential desire is *unnecessary* as a bridge to one's own future, because the connection is already guaranteed by formal conditions on practical reason. But even if it were present, it would not be sufficient to yield serious reasons, simply *because* it is a desire with a future object. I have already expressed doubt that desires are the most important sources of motivation. I now wish to extend this doubt, with particular emphasis, to the case of unmotivated desires with future objects. The reasons for action which they provide are insignificant at best. Since the system under attack demands that desires with future objects should be admitted in general as an important source of reasons, if this can be called in question, the system will be further discredited.

It must be emphasized that I am discussing *unmotivated* desires for the future which are supposed to operate as *sources* of motivation: I am not talking about the motivated pursuit of future goals selected for independent reasons. Nothing is commoner than desires for what is future, but they are nearly always motivated by reasons which will *obtain* in the future, in which case the desires do not originate the motivation. —*too hasty!*

Consider, however, the hypothetical example of a (non-prudential) desire for the future not dependent on any reasons for action which will obtain then. Suppose that for no reason having to do with the future, I conceive now a desire to become a policeman on my 35th birthday. If I do not believe that the desire will persist, or that any circumstances then obtaining will provide me with reason for being or becoming a policeman, is it possible to maintain nevertheless that the desire itself gives me reason to do what will promote its realization? It would be extremely peculiar if anyone allowed himself to be moved to action by such a desire, or regarded it as anything but a nervous symptom to be looked on with suspicion and got rid of as soon as possible. In general, no one wants anything future in this way, without a reason derived from the expectation of a reason.

There are occasional exceptions—whims about minor matters. One does for example find provisions in wills about where the deceased wants his ashes scattered, and it would be stretching a point to argue that this must always be explained in terms of reasons which he thinks will obtain *after his death* for committing his remains to the Potomac. Such a fancy, reaching out from the present to the future, may justify limited measures to ensure its fulfilment, but even if it is very strongly felt, the reasons which it provides are certainly not strong enough to support the extensive array of rational conduct by which ordinary prudential foresight is manifested and which would have to be supported by reasons stemming from an imagined general prudential desire.

I do not claim that it is impossible or incoherent to ascribe to a person significant and powerful, but unmotivated desires with future objects. Any sufficiently directed behaviour permits us to ascribe a desire, and concerted behaviour might in principle be directed at almost any goal. I claim that such desires for the future are rare, and that the reasons they provide are weak at best. The desires may indeed be motivationally unintelligible. And we cannot make unintelligible directed behaviour intelligible by explaining it in terms of an equally unintelligible desire ascribed on the basis of exactly that behaviour.[1]

8. If it appears that the presence of an unmotivated desire for something future is in most cases not a good reason for pursuing that object, doubt is cast on the suggestion that a present desire for future satisfaction or well-being can be the source of reasons for prudential conduct. Even when such desires do provide

---

[1] This is connected with G. E. M. Anscombe's contention that one cannot 'just want' just anything. The reply 'I just wanted to', offered as a *reason* for doing something, has only a very limited application. See *Intention* (Oxford: Blackwell, 1957), pp. 69–71.

reasons they are merely whims, to which it is irrational to attach excessive importance. One *might* for no reason at all conceive a desire that there should be parsley on the moon, and do what one could to smuggle some into the next available rocket; one might simply like the idea. But this is not the alleged status of the proposed prudential desire; it is supposed to be something far more serious than a whim, something which exerts decisive claims on our rational conduct. We do not merely *like* the idea of *Nice* our own future happiness.

The hypothesis might be saved if we could discover something about this particular desire which explains why it provides serious reasons. But there is a much simpler alternative: namely, that something besides a prudential desire lies at the source of prudential reasons, something that accounts for the rationality both of prudential conduct and of prudential desires, which turn out to be motivated as well. All these conditions are met by the structural factor already mentioned. A desire for one's future well-being, unlike certain other desires for the future, is perfectly intelligible, and therefore an apparent candidate for the source of prudential reasons and prudential motivation, because it already *has* perfectly good reason, in the form of its future objects. Desire for the satisfaction of future desires is justified and motivated by reasons which the expectation of such future desires provides. But if we remove the support of such reasons (as we must if we make the desire their basis) then it becomes a detached whim, unworthy of any strong rational influence on conduct.[1]

The structural condition which accounts for prudence is a general one, and does not apply only to reasons stemming from desires. It entails that the influence of reasons can extend over time, because there is reason to *promote* that for which there is *or will be* a reason. The full statement of this condition and its interpretation will occupy the next two chapters, and will require certain general observations about reasons for action beyond those made so far. Its meaning is simple enough, however:

[1] It may be added parenthetically that the same can be said of other desires, including many with present objects. They are often motivated by reasons deriving from their objects, rather than being original sources of reasons and motivation. I have focused on the queerness of desires for the future unaccompanied by reasons stemming from the future, because a desire of that sort plays the crucial role in the theory I am attacking.

the influence of reasons is transmitted over time because reasons represent values which are not time-dependent. One might even describe them as timeless values. So if a given condition creates a reason for something to happen, there is not only a reason to bring that thing about when the condition is present; there is also a reason to promote its future occurrence if the condition is expected to obtain later on. An expected reason is a reason nonetheless.[1]

---

[1] The general principles which yield this consequence imply that the circumstances that create a reason may occur either earlier or later than the time of action. They therefore permit a new understanding of the reasons provided by those whims about the future which we discussed above. A man who buys himself a cemetery plot and the widow who later ensures that he gets into it may be acting for the same reason: namely, the one provided by his original wish to be buried there. Neither of them need believe that a further reason is provided by circumstances obtaining at the time of burial. Revenge and retribution are further examples of reasons which span time; they may not be good reasons, but their form becomes intelligible if we give up the assumption that a reason must always be the product of circumstances existing at the time of action. A substantive account of such backward-looking reasons would of course require more work.

VII

REASONS

1. The condition of timelessness on which prudential motives depend is an aspect of the condition of generality which characterizes all reasons. It is therefore necessary, before arriving at an interpretation of prudence, to characterize this generality condition formally and to explain how prudential reasons arise from it. I shall outline the position in this section, and elaborate it in the remainder of the chapter.

Every reason can be formulated as a predicate. If the predicate applies to some act, event, or circumstance (possible or actual), then there is a reason for that act, event, or circumstance to occur.[1] Such a predicate provides reasons both primarily and derivatively: primarily, for things to which it applies, and derivatively, for things which promote that to which it applies primarily. All the reasons thus provided are only prima facie reasons, and given almost any event for whose occurrence there are prima facie reasons, it will also be possible to discover prima facie reasons for its non-occurrence.

Since it is people who have reasons—to act or to refrain, to promote or to prevent things—the general description of how reasons operate should show this. Let us simplify matters by (1) regarding the failure to do act B as the act of not doing B, (2) treating the prevention of A as the promotion of not-A, and (3) treating the performance of act B as a degenerate case of promoting the occurrence of act B. Then we can say that every reason is a predicate R such that for all persons p and events A, if R is true of A, then p has prima facie reason to promote A.[2]

[1] We do not have to define a separate category of negative reasons, for any predicate P which provides a reason *against* the occurrence of anything to which it applies, will have corresponding to it another predicate Q which provides a reason *for* anything to which it applies, and which covers the same territory. We need only define Q as the predicate which holds of x when P holds of the non-occurrence of x.

[2] 'Events' is of course too narrow a word to cover the scope of A. A can be an act, event, circumstance, state of affairs, and perhaps other things as well. A reason can apply to a specific event, like my turning on the radio ten seconds from now,

It must be mentioned here for future reference that this definition contains no restrictions on the nature of the predicate R. It may for example include a free occurrence of the variable p (what I shall refer to as a free agent-variable.) Thus the most general reason of self-interest could be stated by letting R be the predicate ' . . . is in the interest of p '. The consequence would be that any person p would have prima facie reason to promote any event A which was in his interest. The reason is still universal, although it will not provide everyone with prima facie reasons to promote the same events. The importance of this will emerge later.

It is now possible to say what prudential reasons depend on. The notion of *promoting* an end presents no special problems for the prudential case; the only question is: under what conditions do we have a reason to promote a *future* end? And the answer to that question which entails the validity of prudential reasons is this: we have a reason to promote any event, actual or possible, if it is tenselessly true that at the time of that event, a reason-predicate applies to it. If the event is past, one cannot of course do anything to promote it, but if the event is future this principle has the consequence that one has a present reason to promote it simply because there *will* be a reason for it to happen when it happens, and not because of any further condition which obtains *now*. It is not necessary that the relevant predicate apply to the end at the time of action. So if a condition at time t will create a reason for A, instead of saying that at t there *will* be a reason for A, we should say that there is, tenselessly, a reason for A to occur at t, and derivative reason now to promote its occurrence. To this we need only add that the reason for A to occur at t must exist independently of the acts we may undertake now to promote it.

This solution seems perfectly obvious if we pose the question in its general form: Does a reason apply derivatively to acts which promote an end only if the reason holds of that end at the time of action, or does it also apply if the reason will come true of the end only later?

or to a very general state of affairs, like someone's being in good health. In the latter case, any number of specific events may promote the end. Without pursuing the matter further, let me acknowledge that serious ontological problems might emerge if I tried to specify the range of A more exactly.

If a person believes, for example, that he has reason to obey
the law, he will not suppose that this gives him reason to do
only what will enable him to obey *current* laws, and not what will
enable him to obey future ones. If he eschewed all such measures, and adopted means to obedience only after a law had
actually been passed, even if he knew beforehand that it was
coming, we would probably conclude that his basic reason for
action was more complex. We might conjecture that he regarded
as a reason for doing something that it constituted *unprepared*
obedience to the law. But the same prudential principle would
apply to this reason; he would have to take care *not* to prepare
himself, while remaining always willing to alter his conduct at
a moment's notice.

The hypothesis that the derivative influence of a reason extends only to contemporaneous acts has slightly more plausibility
in the case of reasons stemming from desires—but only because
of the erroneous view, already discussed at length, that a
present desire is required as the basis for every motivation. If
one is convinced that a desire must be present as the source of
every motivation, and that a reason must be capable of providing motivation, one will naturally conclude that desires provide reasons only when they are present, and will organize one's
account of prudence accordingly. I have argued that if desires
are capable of providing reasons at all, then the mere prospect
of a desire may motivate by itself in the same way that the prospect of any other reason may.

Such prudential reasons arise, in short, because if it is tenselessly true that a reason-predicate applies independently to a
certain event—present or future—then there is prima facie
reason to promote that event. To explain this claim it is
necessary to expand on four notions which it employs: the
notion of a prima facie reason, the notion of *promoting* an end,
the notion of *independent* application of a reason-predicate, and
the notion of tenselessness. I shall take them up in that order.

2. Prima facie reasons for particular acts are intermediate between general reasons and particular conclusions as to what
should be done, on the balance of all applicable considerations.
I shall here concern myself solely with the way in which prima
facie reasons are generated, and shall leave aside the question

how conflicts between them are resolved to yield decisive conclusions about what there is sufficient reason to do. This divi-
sion is consciously artificial, and does not imply the view that
practical reasoning actually operates in two successive stages:
first, a listing of all the prima facie reasons (each with its
appropriate weight), then a calculation of how they balance
out.

It may be that such intervening variables can be dispensed
with in a complete system of practical reason, which will perhaps allow the direct derivation of determinate conclusions
about what to do, from the total system of general reasons plus
further information. But at present I have no such system (nor
in real life do we operate consciously with such a system), and
reference to prima facie reasons is necessary to express the partial results that I want to propose.

As for an analysis of the term 'prima facie reason': the present treatment, which assigns it a place in relation to certain
others and describes how prima facie reasons arise and how
they can be derived, may be regarded as itself a partial analysis.
Since my discussion is concerned almost entirely with conditions
from which the presence of prima facie reasons follows, rather
than with what in turn follows from that, the analysis is incomplete. One would seek to complete it by the specification of
principles permitting the derivation of reasons *simpliciter,* sufficient reasons, and decisive conclusions about what should be
done, from premises stating prima facie reasons.

It would clearly not be enough, moreover, to begin with a
mere listing of prima facie reasons, for they are not sufficiently
refined or differentiated to allow any foothold for a balancing
or weighting principle designed to yield specific rational results.
And as I have said, a more complete rational system which
allowed the derivation of decisive results might not have to
operate through the intermediate factor of prima facie reasons
at all, even if they could be weighted appropriately. But given
that I am here intent only on specifying the conditions under
which a given factor or general reason has *any* rational bearing
on a given act at all, I need not concern myself with that
question.

A prima facie reason is simply the minimal rational influence
of a general reason on the appropriateness of a particular action,

and its only decisive consequence is that it becomes a sufficient reason if it is the *only* reason bearing on the matter in question, and if no reasons as strong bear on any alternatives, including the alternative of *not* performing the relevant act. Since this is essentially never the case, mere knowledge of prima facie reasons will be useless in deciding what to do.[1]

3. Something must now be said about what is comprehended under the notion of *promoting* an end. The problem is this: If a person has reason to promote an end A, then there are certain relations which may hold between an act, B, of that person, and the end, A, from which it follows that he has a reason for doing B.[2] What are those relations? One of them is of course identity. Another, which has not yet been defined, is the relation of B's being a *means* to A. There are others as well. I shall begin by discussing the notion of means, and explaining what cases it fails to include.

Perhaps the most important thing about the means-end relation is that it cannot be defined in terms of probability. A means is not just something relative to which the end has a high probability, or a higher probability than it would have in the absence of the means. The means must produce or sustain the end or contribute to its production.[3] For example, the probability of someone's being rich is greater if he wears $300 suits than if he does not, but wearing $300 suits is not a means of getting rich. This is a feature worth retaining in the broader concept of *promoting* an end. But other features entail that the concept of means is too narrow for our purposes.

First, a *logically* necessary condition of the achievement of an

---

[1] The ordinary term 'reason' is restricted to cases in which the factor in question is sufficiently significant to be operative in deliberation, even though it may be outweighed by countervailing reasons. We should not say, for example, that to someone driving a severely injured person to the hospital, the beauty of the scenery along a considerably slower alternative route provides a reason to take it, though that reason is outweighed by the urgency of the circumstances. In those circumstances, beautiful scenery, or the annoyance of leaving a book in the middle of a chapter, are no reason at all for declining to get the person to the hospital as quickly as possible. Yet they will count as prima facie reasons on my definition, simply because they are derivable from appropriate general reasons which apply in this case.

[2] For brevity, I shall often say 'reason' when I mean 'prima facie reason'.

[3] This notion will have to remain undefined.

end cannot naturally be called a means to that end. For example, although the attendance of each member of a philosophy department at a meeting is a condition of 100 per cent attendance, nevertheless the attendance of any one of those members is not a means to 100 per cent attendance. Yet we should say that a member who had reason to promote 100 per cent attendance had thereby reason to attend himself.[1]

But the most serious omission from the class of means is inaction. If one has reason to promote A, one also has reason to refrain from preventing it. So if an act B is a means to the non-occurrence of A, one has reason not to do B. But not doing B would not ordinarily be described as a means to A, simply because doing B was a means to not-A. Nevertheless if the latter condition obtains, it follows that if one has reason to promote A, one has reason not to do B.

The results so far may be summarized as follows: If a person has reason to promote A, that gives him reason to do B if B bears any of the following relations to A: (1) B is identical with A; (2) B will produce, sustain, or contribute to the production or sustention of A; (3) B is a logically necessary condition of A;[2] (4) B consists in not doing C, and C bears any of relations (1), (2), or (3) to the non-occurrence of A.

But of course this can only be the beginning of the matter, for there will often be countless acts available to a single individual, bearing one of these relations to a given end. (Many will be incompatible or redundant.) One requires in addition a method of ordering all these acts (or perhaps sets of them) in respect of their suitability as ways of promoting the end. In fact, a mere ordering will be insufficient; ideally one needs a method of calculating the relative strength of the reasons for doing each of them. Those relative strengths should govern the settlement of conflicts between different primary reasons in their application to a single act. But I shall restrict myself to stating sufficient conditions for the presence of prima facie reasons for action, and for that purpose the general notion of promoting an end is good enough.

---

[1] A logically sufficient condition for an end does not count as a means either, but that is just as well; P & Q is a logically sufficient condition for Q, but a reason to do P is not a reason to do P & Q (unless one cannot do P without doing Q).

[2] (3) includes (1).

4. The third matter to be explained in this account of derivative reasons is that the existence of the conditions which provide the tenseless primary reason for an end must not be dependent on the occurrence of the acts to which that reason applies derivatively. That is, to have a reason to promote an end, one must expect that there will be a reason for it whether one undertakes to promote the end or not. In this way we eliminate cases in which a single act both creates a problem for the future and then contributes to its solution. For example, if I remove the door of my office from its hinges I shall be in possession of a door to install in the now doorless entrance to my office. But the reason for possessing such an unattached door will not exist independently of my adopting this measure, so removing the door does not promote an end for which there is going to be a reason independently.

Of course we sometimes have a reason to do what will simultaneously promote an end and provide the reason for that end; as when one learns to play squash because, having learned, one will enjoy playing, and will be able to play for enjoyment. Here the future end is playing squash, the future reason is that it will be enjoyable, the present means is learning to play squash; and the future reason for playing squash is not going to exist unless the means is undertaken. One will not enjoy playing unless one learns how.

However, in this case, as in all such cases, there is an independent additional reason for promoting the existence of that future reason, i.e., for promoting the enjoyability of squash. Independently of the actual undertaking of the means, there will be reason in the future, as there always is, to want to be capable of deriving pleasure from as many harmless activities as possible (whereas there is no reason to bring it about that one needs a door to one's office). Therefore in learning to play squash one does promote an end for which there is independent reason; one increases the possibility of enjoyment.

There appear to be three types of case: (1) cases in which one has reason to promote an end if the reason holds or will hold of that end, but no reason either to promote or to prevent the *existence* of that reason; (2) cases in which one has reason to promote an end if the reason holds or will hold of that end, and also reason to promote the existence of that reason (this is true when the reason is a reward); (3) cases in which one has reason actually to *prevent* a certain reason from existing (as is true in the case of penalties), although if it does hold or will hold one has reason to promote that to which it applies.[1] In cases of type (2), one has reason to promote the likelihood of the conjunction of the presence of the reason and that to which it applies. In cases of type (3), one has reason to do what will reduce the likelihood of the conjunction of the presence of the reason and the non-occurrence of that to which it applies. None of these cases contravenes the condition that the primary reason for an end must exist independently of the measures taken to promote it.

5. The condition which is crucial for prudence is that a reason-predicate need apply only tenselessly to create derivative reasons. If at the time of an event the predicate applies to it, there is tenselessly a reason to promote the event's occurrence at that time, by action at that or any prior time.[2]

Now it may be objected that a merely tenseless truth about a future time is not necessarily true in the present. For example, it may be true on 15 May that there is an airline strike. But it may not yet be true on 1 May that on 15 May there *will* be an airline strike, and in that case how can it be even tenselessly true *on 1 May* that there is an airline strike on 15 May? And if that is not true on 1 May, how can it create a reason on 1 May to arrange alternative land transportation to Chicago for 15 May?

There are two ways of dealing with this difficulty. (a) One can say that in such a case there *is* a tenseless truth about the future and a derivative reason for action in the present, but a prospective agent has no way of knowing this except through the kind of evidence which would justify him in believing a future tense statement about the airline strike; consequently he has a reason to arrange alternative transportation but cannot know it—or (b) one can say that the agent has no reason to

[1] Cf. Robert Nozick, 'Coercion', in *Philosophy, Science, and Method: Essays in Honor of Ernest Nagel*, ed. Morgenbesser, Suppes, and White (New York, 1969).

[2] Or even at a future time—for someone who thinks he can affect the past. In any case there will be reason subsequently to *want* the event to have occurred, even if one can no longer do anything about it.

promote an end until it is true that the reason-predicate holds
or will hold of that end. Alternative (b) amounts to an interpretation of tenseless truth as truth in any of the three major
tenses. It is not an abandonment of the timelessness of reasons
because although the conditions which confer a reason on an
event have been conceded not to be timeless, the value which
that reason embodies is still timeless, and can transmit its influence from future to past, once it is clear that the reason will
be present. We may therefore continue to speak of timeless
reasons, and the tenselessness of their conditions, without
deciding between the two interpretations offered above.

But two further questions grow out of this initial one. The first
is that, even if no true prediction can be made about the future
occurrence of a certain condition, it is often possible to assign a
probability to that occurrence, and such probabilities enter into
practical reasoning. For example it may be that on 1 May there
is an even chance of an airline strike on 15 May, and this creates
reasons for action related to those which are created by the
definite prediction of a strike.

I do not propose to go into this matter at all—not because it
is unimportant, but because it is a perfectly general problem
about practical reason, and not a problem specifically about
prudential motives. Even when a reason-predicate applies
unequivocally to a *present* situation, probabilities may enter into
the choice of an act best suited to promote the desired end.
Different means have different probabilities of success. When
the end is future, probabilities affect the status of the end as well
as the choice of methods to promote it, but this is just the extension of a feature which permeates practical reasoning, and which
is best treated in the context of a general systematic theory of
decision.

Similar considerations prevent me from attempting a solution to the final problem, which is this: How do *beliefs* about
future conditions, as opposed to the tenseless *truth* about those
conditions, affect what prudential reasons one has for present
action? Whether or not there will be an airline strike on 15 May,
one may believe that there will, and hence believe that it is
tenselessly true that an airline strike occurs on 15 May. One
will therefore *believe* that one has certain prudential reasons to
prepare alternatives, but *does* one therefore have such reasons?

This question again is perfectly general, and can arise in regard to any kind of reason. If it has a solution when the reason is present, that same solution will apply to the case in which the primary reason is future.

In any case, these problems do not threaten the hypothesis that reasons are timeless. For if we wish to introduce beliefs or probabilities into the conditions for prudential reasons, that which is believed or that which is probable will be simply that conditions exist for the presence of timeless reasons. I maintain that the failure to regard all reasons as timeless involves one in a peculiar sort of dissociation from one's practical concerns. That claim will be defended in the next chapter.

VIII

THE INTERPRETATION OF PRUDENTIAL REASONS: IDENTITY OVER TIME

1. It is important to provide an *interpretation* of the prudential constraints on practical reason, because without such an explanation, what has been said so far is only a piece of descriptive motivational psychology, and not a specification of genuine rational requirements on action. It does not of course describe what people actually do, since they do not always follow the counsels of prudence. Rather it is in part a description of how people behave, and in part a systematic account of certain intuitions about how they *should* behave: intuitions that certain considerations are relevant to a decision and others irrelevant, intuitions about the adequacy of certain justifications and the effectiveness of certain criticisms of action.

Now these intuitions, and their influence on action, could be set forth systematically, and the result might even have the form of a normative system, for the characteristic expression of such responses has a normative form. But if the matter is taken no further than that, we shall be left without any theory about the *object* of those intuitions, the requirements themselves. Of course we cannot exclude in advance the possibility that these particular intuitions *have* no independent objects, that they are not to be taken as indications of something further, which accounts for their presence and supports their validity, and of which they may be regarded as perceptions. But the opposite view, that such intuitions are objective and possess an explanation which supports their validity, is also possible, and I propose to defend it. The issue is familiar from ethics: do our intuitions of moral requirements on action have any objective basis, or are they *mere* intuitions, internally consistent but without objects?[1]

[1] In a larger sense this is a general problem of scepticism: are we to regard our organized intuitive responses to the world as evidence of a corresponding objective organization which we perceive, or must objectivity always be defined in terms of the responses themselves?

The account which I shall propose, in the present case as in the later case of altruism, is a metaphysical one. This is not to be taken in a Platonic sense; I do not suggest that the objectivity of altruistic or prudential requirements could be guaranteed by the contents of a super-sensible realm, which we perceive when our practical intuitions are correct. The metaphysics to which I shall appeal is a metaphysics of the person, and it will support the objective validity of prudential constraints by interpreting them as the practical expression of an awareness that one persists over time. Those practical intuitions which acknowledge prudential reasons, and the motives connected with them, reflect an individual's conception of himself as a temporally persistent being: his ability to identify with past and future stages of himself and to regard them as forming a single life. Failure to be susceptible to prudence entails radical dissociation from one's future, one's past, and from oneself as a whole, conceived as a temporally extended individual.

2. In the following discussion I shall employ the notion of a dated reason in contrast with that of a timeless one. Timeless reasons transmit their influence over time in the way described in the previous chapter. A dated reason, on the other hand, supports action to promote a given end only if the reason-predicate can be ascribed to that end in the *present* tense at the time of action. I shall try to explain why the acceptance only of dated reasons indicates a failure to identify with one's future self—and even, in a curious sense, with one's present self. Let us begin by considering an example.

Suppose I shall be in Rome six weeks from now; then in six weeks, I shall have reason to speak Italian. If I regard this only as a dated reason, then, even granted my present ignorance of the language, I cannot conclude that I now have reason to enrol in an Italian course, since my reason for speaking Italian will not come into existence for six more weeks. I am forced instead to wait for its arrival, fatalistically, as for the onset of the effects of a drug—wait for it to galvanize me into action.

Suppose that, true to my rational principles, I allow the six weeks to go by without learning Italian. Having managed somehow to board a plane (we may imagine that my prudential block is not complete), I contemplate the reason's approach with detached curiosity while crossing the Atlantic. The plane lands; I descend the gangway, collect my luggage, hail a cab, and suddenly it is upon me: I cannot tell the driver where I want to go. Presumably I shall be frustrated and vexed; I shall gesture, try to improvise, perhaps excuse myself briefly to purchase a phrase book at the airport news-stand.

One important reaction *not* open to me is regret, so long as I continue to regard my reasons for speaking Italian as dated and as having suddenly come into force. I cannot reflect now that I should have learned Italian while I had the chance, for when I had the chance, I did not have the reason. I may wish that I had enrolled in a course, but I cannot regard my present dated reasons for speaking Italian as reasons for having learned it earlier. Thus dated reasons represent a peculiar attitude even when they are operative, and not only when they are projected. Someone who predicts dated reasons for future action is dissociated from his future concerns, but someone who acts on a dated reason is detached from his present concerns, for he thinks they are of no concern to other stages of himself.

Now one might say that an individual who behaves in this way is *ipso facto* guilty of failure to identify with his future and past self—that susceptibility to prudential motives is part of what it *is* so to identify, or is among the criteria of such identification. But this, while not entirely incorrect, would make the matter seem much simpler than it is, and might even suggest that it depended on linguistic convention. In fact, it is possible to explain the connection precisely, and when that has been done it will become clear in what sense susceptibility to prudence is among the criteria for identification with one's future. This task requires that we arrive at a more precise account of what it is to regard oneself as a person who persists over time: specifically what it is to identify with that person at stages other than the present. Otherwise such identification cannot be connected rigorously with the acceptance of timeless reasons. The formal analysis will corroborate and explain what we are naturally inclined to say about the behaviour of someone who relies on dated reasons, and it will in fact emerge that the idea that one is temporally extended depends on a certain view of the present.

In the next section I shall discuss temporal identification and dissociation in general, without special reference to the issues of practical reason. What emerges will be used subsequently for the precise interpretation of timeless reasons.

3. In discussing the influence of reasons over time, it is necessary to consider various types of dissociation: dissociation from one's future self, from one's past self, from oneself as a persisting individual—even dissociation from one's present self. All of them, and the identifications to which they are opposed, can be described by reference to the conception of oneself as a temporally extended person.

To identify with one's past or future is simply to regard the present as a stage in the life of a persisting individual, of which those other times are also (earlier or later) stages. We may therefore omit a separate treatment of identifications with past and future, and concentrate instead on how one identifies the present with a point in the life of a temporally extended person.

The idea of a temporally persistent human being is an exceedingly complicated one, and many philosophical problems can be raised about it which are not immediately relevant to the present issue: problems about the conditions for re-identification of any particulars over time, as well as specific problems about personal identity, and the degree to which an individual may change without becoming another person. What will concern us, however, is an extremely abstract feature of the conception —one which has more to do with time in general than with personal identity. It is the condition that a person be equally real at all stages of his life; specifically, the fact that a particular stage is *present* cannot be regarded as conferring on it any special status. This is a truism, for every stage of one's life is present sooner or later; so all times are on an equal footing in that regard. But the truism must be explicated, and we must attempt to explain how the view that all times of one's life are equally real fits together with the view that a particular one of them is now present.

In order to concentrate on these matters, let us assume that there is a more or less coherent conception, which can be possessed without analysis, of an individual human being who lives for a number of years and can be re-identified at different times and places as the same person. What, beyond this, is involved in according equal status to different times?

The further factor needed to complete the conception is a belief that what can be asserted significantly of the present can be asserted significantly of other times also, and can be true or false of those times in the same sense in which it is true or false of the present. The present is just a time among others, and confers no special status on the circumstances which occupy it. This means not only that what can be asserted or believed of the present can be asserted or believed in the same sense of the future or the past, but also that what can be asserted of the present in the present tense could have been asserted of it in the same sense earlier or later, using the future or past tense. And any prediction about the future is of something which will be statable in the present tense when the future actually appears. In sum, the sense of an assertion about what is the case at a certain time does not change with the tense of the assertion; the tense merely indicates a relation between the time of utterance and the time of what is being talked about.

The category of a *tenseless* statement has been devised to express what is asserted in common by past, present, and future statements about the same circumstance or state of affairs. The conditions for the correctness of a tensed statement can then be divided into two parts: (a) a tenseless truth about the time which is the subject of the statement; and (b) a relation between that time and the time of utterance which makes the tense employed the appropriate one. Thus, if someone predicts that I shall break my leg tomorrow, his statement is correct only if (a) I break my leg on a certain day, and (b) the statement is made on the previous day. Moreover if he believes the prediction he is committed to accepting the other two statements (though I do not claim that the first statement can be *analysed* into the other two, or that conscious formulation of the latter is implied by belief of the former). This applies to all tensed statements, the present tense included. Any circumstance describable from one temporal standpoint can also be described from the others, and a tenseless statement expresses what is asserted in common by these alternative descriptions.

Tenseless statements therefore provide us with the means of expression appropriate to a standpoint of temporal neutrality towards the events of our lives. We can of course also regard those events from a tensed standpoint, and we usually do. But the possibility of viewing them tenselessly must always be available. To regard oneself as a being who persists through time, one must regard the facts of one's past, present, and future life as tenselessly specifiable truths about different times in the history of a being with the appropriate kind of temporal continuity. And one must be able to regard the present as merely one of those times.

The employment of tensed statements is compatible with this condition, so long as any tensed assertion or belief is acknowledged to imply a tenseless statement about the same subject, plus the existence of a condition which makes the relevant tense appropriate.[1] Any tensed statements which cannot be assimilated to this conception suggest the existence of an area in which the sense of one's equal reality over time is defective. In so far as one nevertheless continues *in general* to possess a sense of temporal persistence, one will remain, from the standpoint of temporal neutrality, dissociated from considerations in the defective area.[2]

[1] It should be noticed that one can adopt a standpoint of temporal neutrality not only towards the matter with which a tensed statement deals, but also towards the tensed statement itself, and the condition which makes the tense appropriate.

[2] It may be objected that this view is incompatible with the existence of future contingencies, and for that reason it is necessary to enlarge briefly on the question—if only to explain that I do not intend to propound a thesis strong enough to settle it. It may be thought that a view of the world and one's life as developing in definiteness over time, with certain parts of the future fixed in advance and others not fixed until they happen or not until shortly before, could be expressed only in tensed terms, and hence could not be accommodated to the condition of a temporally neutral, tenseless point of view. This would be important, for since our concern is ultimately the theory of action and reasons for action, it would be a radical step to rule out at this point of the discussion any possibility that there are such things as future contingencies. We ought at least to leave that question unsettled, if possible.

In fact, however, a tenseless system is perfectly capable of accommodating these distinctions. Any defender of future contingencies presumably believes that they are predictions whose truth or falsity is not determined by present circumstances, and he must believe, by contrast, that there are ways in which present or past circumstances *can* determine the future. There seems no reason to believe that such a relation cannot be expressed tenselessly. If we can say, 'It is now definite that there will be a meeting tomorrow', we can also say, 'It was not definite until yesterday afternoon that there would be a meeting today.' Why then can we not say (tenselessly), 'It is definite after t_1, but not before, that there is a meeting at t_2'? In general any tensed claim made at t_1 that a circumstance at t_2 is definite, will be true if and only if, tenselessly, the circumstance obtains at t_2, and either t_2 is earlier than or identical with t_1, or else (tenselessly) circumstances up to t_1 include sufficient conditions for the occurrence of the circumstance at t_2. (What constitute

4. I shall now attempt to apply these observations to the real
subject of our investigation—namely practical reasoning and
the judgments involved in it. I contend that one can ask of a
practical principle or a reason for action whether it is consistent
with the conception of oneself as a person extended in time, or
whether the acceptance of it must be dissociated from that conception. Some principles and reasons are in accord with the
conception, but others, I believe, are not, for their acceptance
is not compatible with the neutrality of viewpoint towards
different times whose possibility I have argued is essential.

Practical judgments will often include or depend on judgments about what is the case. To the extent that this is so, they
are subject to the conditions already discussed. Consider the
judgment that I shall have a reason to speak Italian in six
weeks. If that is true, it is true because in six weeks I shall find
myself in a situation which provides a reason for speaking
Italian, according to a practical principle which holds at all
times. And since the prediction of that situation is merely a
statement about the future which asserts of it something which
could also be asserted tenselessly, it follows that the prediction
of the reason is correct only if (a) certain conditions (tenselessly)
obtain at the relevant time, which yield a reason according to a
tenselessly specifiable principle, and (b) that time is six weeks
later than the time of my prediction. The same can be said of
practical judgments in the present tense.

However, the matter becomes complicated when we consider
that a practical judgment is more than a judgment that certain
conditions obtain or will obtain, which bring the relevant course
of action under general practical principles. The reasons for a
practical judgment are reasons for *doing* or *wanting* something,
and not just reasons for believing something. Therefore the
judgment that I shall have reason to speak Italian in six weeks

---

sufficient conditions will depend on the particular theory of the defender of future
contingencies.) But this is a perfectly tenseless definition of future contingency and
its opposite.

Therefore the requirement that every tensed statement should have tenselessly
specifiable truth conditions does not rule out the possibility of future contingencies,
predictions of which, though not yet true at one time, may become true later on.
We have only to construe the predictions as assertions of the present *definiteness* of
the thing predicted, instead of mere assertions that it will occur (which are presumably true if and only if (tenselessly) it does).

is a judgment that certain acts or desires on my part will be *justified* at that time.

If this were merely a further claim about what will be the case at the time with which the practical judgment deals, it could be easily assimilated to the neutral standpoint by the introduction of tenseless justification-statements, whose truth would be among the conditions of correctness for any tensed practical claim. But it is not as simple as that, because a judgment that a certain action or desire is justified has motivational content. To accept a reason for doing something is to accept a reason for *doing* it, not merely for *believing* that one should do it. If it is to be possible to make practical judgments from a standpoint of temporal neutrality then this practical aspect must be a feature of tenseless as well as of present tense judgments. And the motivational content which is common to a present tense practical judgment and its tenseless counterpart will also be common to future and past tense judgments to the same effect, made at different times about that same situation.

Precisely the issue under consideration, of course, is whether a practical judgment about what one will have reason to do in the *future* carries with it any potential commitment to act, or to desire. So it is important not to beg the question. But I hope to establish that this type of motivational content must be present in all practical judgments, by first considering what is true of present tense judgments and then applying the requirement of temporal neutrality to this. In that way it will be possible to derive consequences for practical judgments about the future, for tenseless judgments, and even for judgments about the past.

As I have said, the crucial point is that a practical reason is a reason to do or want something, as a theoretical reason is a reason to conclude or believe something. This is the defining characteristic of practical reasoning. To hold, as Hume did, that the only proper rational criticism of action is a criticism of the beliefs associated with it, is to hold that practical reason does not exist. If we acknowledge the existence of reasons for action we must hold not merely that they justify us in believing certain special propositions about action, but rather that they justify action itself. It must be possible to engage in rational criticism of action and desire, rather than just of the beliefs associated with them. A first person, present tense practical judgment about what one should do is not merely a belief. It is not, of course, an action either. But to be led by certain reasons to such a judgment is to accept those reasons as a justification for doing or wanting that which it is judged one should do or want.

If the practical judgment did not itself possess this motivational content, then a further argument would be necessary to justify action or desire, *given* the practical judgment. That is, even if one had arrived at the practical judgment that there was reason to act, this would give no reason to *act*: one could go on to ask, 'Why do what I have a reason to do?' And if that question remained open, then the practical judgment under consideration would not after all be the conclusion of the process of practical reasoning: the reasons supporting it would be reasons for belief only, and not reasons for action. In that case the possibility of genuine practical reasoning would depend on the availability of a further argument whose conclusion possessed genuine motivational content. Now such a further step *might* be available, and if so, then it would have to be added to the original argument to complete the practical reasoning to its desired conclusion. But if practical reasoning exists at all, it is natural to suppose that the motivational content of its conclusions is present in ordinary practical judgments to begin with. Hence I contend that the judgment that one has reason to do something includes the acceptance of a justification for doing it, and that this is its motivational content.

A more exact description of this content presents difficulties, for motivational content does not necessarily imply motivational efficacy. It is undeniable that someone may acknowledge a reason for action and fail to act. Indefinitely many circumstances may explain this. Indeed, I believe that a practical judgment can sometimes fail to prompt action or desire without any explanation. Not every case of irrational behaviour need be comprehensible. But in what sense can a judgment possess motivational content if its motivational efficacy can be blocked in indefinitely many ways?

One way in which the effects of a reason may be blocked, of course, is by countervailing reasons, but this need not cause difficulty. If an acknowledged reason is only a prima facie reason then it will carry with it only prima facie justification. And if the motivational content of acknowledgments of *sufficient* reasons for action can be understood, then it should be possible to account for the motivational content of present tense judgments about prima facie reasons in terms of their capacity to support more conclusive judgments about sufficient reasons. Let us therefore consider the latter type of judgment.

In a judgment of sufficient practical reason for an act, countervailing reasons have already been accommodated. There remain various other causes of failure to be inclined accordingly; many of these, though not all, come under the heading of weakness of will before one temptation or another. If there is an adequate explanation, then it will reveal how the motivational effectiveness of the practical conviction has been blocked or undermined. Weakness, cowardice, laziness, panic are all factors of this type, and each represents a subtle variety of motivational interference. Therefore the fact that appropriate action or desire may be prevented in these ways does not cast doubt on the claim that a judgment of practical reason possesses motivational weight. Indeed it is possible for a man to be in certain respects *consistently* weak or cowardly, so that he rarely acts in accord with his practical convictions about a certain matter: alcohol, for example.

Cases where no explanation of the failure is available are more difficult, but here too some conditions must be met if failure is not to cast doubt on the genuineness of conviction expressed by the ineffective practical judgment. If such judgments are too frequent—if without explanation an individual rarely or never acts on practical judgments adducing the presence of a certain type of reason—then we shall conclude that he is merely paying lip-service to the view that it is a reason, and does not really accept it as such. If on the other hand such lapses are only occasional, then there may be enough connection with motivation to permit us to credit the genuineness of the conviction. To cover such attenuated cases, it might be best to say that if someone arrives at a practical judgment and no contrary influences are operative, that judgment *can* by itself motivate him to the appropriate act or desire, and usually does. Either he or someone else can offer the judgment and its grounds as a sufficient explanation of his action, without a further account of why it prompted him to act.[1]

In general, therefore, the motivational content of a judgment of sufficient practical reason is quite clear; and the cases in which it is less clear must be understood against a background of related cases in which the motivational weight can be seen, if only through the influences necessary to overcome it. If this is true, it permits us to formulate a description of the motivational component, which is compatible with all the possibilities of failure in actual motivation without thereby becoming empty. The belief that a reason provides me with sufficient justification for a present course of action does not necessarily imply a desire or a willingness to undertake that action; it is not a sufficient condition of the act or desire. But it is sufficient, in the absence of contrary influences, to *explain* the appropriate action, or the desire or willingness to perform it.[2] That is the motivational content of a judgment about what one presently has reason to do.

Although I believe that this account is roughly correct, it is not essential that it should be agreed to as it stands. What is essential for my argument is that a practical judgment about what one has reason to do now should be acknowledged to possess *some* motivational content. The content I have suggested may be considered weak. My concern is that it or something like it should seem plausible to anyone who believes that reasons can motivate when they are acknowledged to be present—even if he denies that they can motivate when they are expected for the future. When one judges that there is *now* a reason to do something, one is not merely judging that certain conditions obtain, or that because of these conditions a certain act can be subsumed under a general principle; in addition one accepts the reason as a justification for acting. The question is whether the requirement of temporal neutrality can be applied to this aspect of our practical judgments, and if so, what the consequences are.

[1] This is equally true of justifications of belief. A belief can be explained by its justification, but it is possible that on occasion someone should regard certain reasons as justifying a belief yet fail to hold it—without our being able to find any further explanation of this. I realize that some of these remarks may contravene certain theories of explanation, but I shall not pursue that issue here.

[2] I do not wish to imply, however, that *whenever* the judgment and the appropriate act occur together, the former explains the latter. The act may on occasion have a quite different cause.

5. It should be possible to accommodate practical judgments to the standpoint of temporal neutrality, because such judgments can be made in different tenses, and about different times. The condition is met by ordinary beliefs, because any belief expressible in tensed terms, about what is the case at a given time, commits one to a tenseless belief about what is the case at that time, plus a belief about the relation between that time and the present. One can specify a perfectly analogous condition on the acceptance of tensed practical judgments, and specifically on tensed acknowledgments of justification. The condition is this: Anyone who accepts a tensed practical judgment about what he has reason to do at a given time must accept (a) a tenseless practical judgment to the same effect about that time and (b) a belief about the relation between that time and the present, which renders appropriate the particular tense employed. If a type of practical judgment does not meet this condition, then it cannot be said that a future-tense claim of that type expresses the same judgment about the time with which it is concerned, as is expressed by the corresponding present-tense claim, made at that time, or by the corresponding past-tense claim, made at a later time. If claims of different tenses about the same time are to express the same judgment about that time, then there must be something common to them all, and the differences between them must not be differences in what they say *about the time with which they deal*, but rather differences in the relation between that time and the time at which they are made, which render appropriate the differences of tense.

This has important consequences. I have argued that a present-tense practical judgment possesses motivational content —namely the acknowledgment of a justification for promoting a certain end. But if this is granted, then acceptance of such a present-tense judgment requires (a) acceptance of a tenseless judgment about the time in question, to the same effect, *including* acknowledgment of a justification for promoting the relevant end, tenselessly specified; and (b) a belief that the time is now, making the present tense appropriate. Moreover a commitment to that same tenseless judgment is also carried by a future-tense judgment to the same effect, made earlier. Both the judgment 'I now have reason to speak Italian', and the judgment (made six weeks earlier) 'In six weeks I shall have reason to speak Italian', commit one to a single tenseless judgment about the time in question: i.e. that at that time there is (tenselessly) reason to speak Italian. And that judgment possesses the motivational content possessed by the present tense version: an acknowledgment that action to promote my ability to speak Italian then is justified.

I realize that this is a strong result. But it depends on two assumptions which, although themselves rather strong, seem difficult to contest. One is the assumption that present-tense practical judgments have motivational content (and the argument will work equally well for some other motivational content than the one suggested, if an alternative should seem more acceptable). The other is the assumption that practical judgments, like other kinds of judgments, are consonant with the conception of oneself as a temporally extended being for whom the future is no less real than the present. This conception requires that one be able to view all times, including the present, from a standpoint of temporal neutrality. Any type of judgment which cannot be accommodated to that standpoint can be accepted only at the cost of dissociation from one's temporally extended self.

Even if the result stands, however, there is the following difficulty. It is evident that the motivational *effects* of a given tenseless practical judgment will vary with one's temporal relation to the circumstance being considered. Whether that circumstance is past, present, or future will bear not only on the appropriateness of formulating practical judgments in a certain tense, but also on what those judgments lead me to do—for what can be done to promote an end depends on one's temporal relation to it, among other things. If the subject of the judgment lies in the past, then unless I have strange views about causation it can motivate me only to *want* something to have happened, or to hope that I have done something, or to regret that I have not. And if I had no inkling of my temporal situation, I should be unable to act no matter how detailed were the tenseless practical conclusions at my disposal. So the possibility of *acting* on a practical judgment depends on an acknowledgment of one's temporal location. Does this show that practical judgments are *necessarily* dissociated from the tenseless standpoint,

and hence from the conception of oneself as temporally extended? That would make it pointless to argue for certain types
of practical reason on the ground that they avoid such
dissociation.

The solution to this difficulty can be seen if we turn to the
case of factual statements, for the same problem arises there.
One does not know what evidence to look for in support of a
tenseless assertion about the burning down of one's house, unless one knows whether the time being referred to is past,
present, or future. If it is past one looks for ashes; if present, for
flames; if future, for an arsonist or a short-circuit. Nevertheless
all of the connections, between the burning of a house and the
phenomena that provide evidence of it, can be specified tenselessly in their turn. When a house burns, the result is usually
ashes, and ashes have a certain look and smell. So a tenseless
belief about the burning down of my house commits me to a
tenseless belief that certain experiences would attend my subsequent arrival on the scene. My temporal relation to the burning determines only whether I expect those experiences now or
later. A corresponding connection exists between my experiences
and the tense of the judgment for which they provide evidence.

Therefore although it is not possible to assess the experiential
evidence for a tensed factual judgment without knowing one's
temporal relation to the circumstance with which the judgment
deals, it is nevertheless possible to specify tenselessly all the
relations of evidence on which such a judgment depends, so that
tenseless conclusions could be drawn on the basis of tenseless
specifications of the evidence. Neither the content of a tensed
judgment nor its evidential connections are inaccessible from a
temporally neutral standpoint: only the tense itself requires
abandonment of that standpoint.

The case is similar with a practical judgment. Although one
cannot act on it unless one knows how the present is related to
the time with which it deals, one can accept the conclusion
nonetheless. That is, given a tenseless specification of the circumstances which provide a reason for action, one can conclude
that a certain act should be undertaken. This judgment possesses motivational content, for one then regards the undertaking
as justified, and this is sufficient to explain one's wanting it to
happen, be happening, or have happened. Such a desire will

form even if one does not know what time it is. Information about one's temporal location merely tells one whether the opportunity of acting on this conclusion is available. If the time in question is present, one can act directly; if it is still to come, the motivation may lead one to take preparatory measures (which can also be justified tenselessly); if it has passed, one may feel hope, fear, regret, or satisfaction, depending on the circumstances. But motivational content is already present in the tenseless judgment. Otherwise the added information that the time in question is present could not of itself lead to action: it would require in addition a practical principle formulable only in the present tense, justifying action if there is a reason to act *now*. And that would mean that practical reasoning was thoroughly dissociated from the standpoint of temporal neutrality. One would be able to arrive from that standpoint only at motivationally empty judgments about the presence of 'justifications' for action, whereas their acceptance as *practical* justifications would depend on a present-tense reformulation of the conditions.

My basic contention has been that practical judgments must share with factual judgments the property of being assimilable to the standpoint of temporal neutrality. Just as a change from a tenseless to a tensed factual judgment does not alter what is believed, but only the standpoint from which one views it, so the change from a tenseless to a tensed practical judgment does not alter what one accepts a justification for wanting, but only the standpoint from which one wants it. If the sense of practical judgments were changed, or their motivational content lost, when one shifted out of the present tense, then practical reasoning would be an area divorced from the conception of oneself as equally real over time.[1]

6. This argument supports the claim that prudence depends on a belief in the reality of the future, and on a conception of oneself as temporally extended. For prudence depends on the

---

[1] I owe to Bernard Williams the observation that when someone says "Thank god that's over", about a disaster that is past, his reaction cannot be entirely expressed from a temporally neutral standpoint. But I believe that insofar as this feeling provides reasons for action, those reasons will be timeless: viz., reasons to accept inevitable suffering without too much delay, thereby shortening the pains of anticipation.

acceptance of timeless rather than dated reasons; and dated reasons entail dissociation, while timeless reasons do not.

This is easily seen. Unless a dated reason is acknowledged to be present, it has no motivational content. Therefore either it lacks motivational content entirely, or it cannot be applied to other times (nor even to the present, tenselessly conceived), in the sense in which it is applied in the present tense. In that case the statement 'In six weeks I shall have reason to speak Italian' does not express the same judgment about that time as the statement 'I now have reason to speak Italian', made six weeks later.

Timeless reasons, on the other hand, avoid dissociation because they permit the tenseless formulation of practical judgments, complete with motivational content. That allows us to make the same practical judgment about a single situation from different temporal standpoints and in different tenses. It also allows the same judgment to be made about two different times, without a shift of sense.

Furthermore, timeless reasons explain the phenomenon of wanting something *to have happened*, simply because there was reason for it in the past. Someone who was too drunk at last night's party to remember what happened will hope that he behaved with restraint—not only because of the subsequent disagreeable effects of idiotic behaviour, but because there was reason to avoid it *then*. (It would be only a partial consolation if everyone else at the party forgot his behaviour completely.) Such desires about the past are appropriate even if one knows what has happened. Regret is to the past as prudence is to the future; both are justified by timeless reasons.

Although I do not wish to present a detailed account of the prudential constraints which follow from the condition of timelessness, a few comments are in order. The condition is not as strict as may initially appear.

For one thing, it is essentially a second order condition, governing the extent of derivative influence exercised by primary reasons which are assumed to be given. It cannot therefore define the primary pursuits of a rational human life, and must not be permitted to dominate the original reasons whose extended influence it accounts for. For example, prudential cares about the satisfaction of future desires cannot be permitted to interfere hopelessly with the spontaneous satisfaction of present desires and impulses. If one made the effort to live at every moment in the service of reasons derived from all other times in one's life, one would fail to live a proper life at all.

Spontaneity and immediacy are of value in themselves, and that does not conflict with the condition of timelessness, for like all other values, they are themselves subject to that condition. If spontaneity is a good, then one has reason to ensure that there will be spontaneity in one's future, not only in the present. Even the most extreme devotee of carefree decisions should be susceptible to the prudential argument that a spontaneous present act which may be very tempting (shooting a policeman, joining the Marines) can seriously diminish his capacity for spontaneous action later on.[1]

Moreover the simple uncertainty of future needs, desires, and circumstances and the constant possibility of death provide additional arguments against excessive planning, despite the fact that reasons are timeless. Present needs are known with greater specificity than future ones. All these factors will prevent the domination of present considerations by long-term ones in our prudential calculations.

Finally, we must consider that a person's values often change over time, and that this may limit the applicability of prudential considerations to some degree. Prudential reasons make

[1] Since the condition of timelessness applies to all reasons, and not only to those which define one's interests in the usual sense, this view may seem to imply that all practical reasoning is consequentialist or teleological; i.e. that it always consists in calculating how much good or bad will be produced by a given act. And if this were a consequence of the requirement of timelessness, it would cast doubt on that requirement, for there may be reasons for action which are not teleological but deontological—which express not the value of some *effect* of action but the rightness or wrongness of the action itself (which is not supposed to be equivalent to the action's value as a possible effect). This at least has been alleged to characterize certain moral reasons; for example, it may be wrong to murder, even in order to prevent other murders, and if this is so, then the wrongness of murder cannot derive simply from its badness. However, the condition of timelessness does not exclude this possibility. It implies only that if murder is always wrong, and never justifiable by its consequences, then it is also something which there is always a timeless reason to prevent. That does not mean that the wrongness of murder is a consequence of the reason for preventing its occurrence—on the contrary, the reverse may be true. And it does not entail that murder may be permissible if its consequences include the prevention of other murders. There may be deontological reasons which have complete priority over any reasons stemming from consequences, including consequences involving other acts of the type in question.

allowance for changing *preferences*, because if for example my preferences in food will be different in the future from what they are now, I shall have reason to eat different things then and consequently I have reason now to put myself into a position to satisfy those future preferences. But this involves not a change in the basic reason—a reason to eat what one likes rather than what one dislikes—but merely a change in the data (one's preferences) which combine with that principle to yield reasons for specific action. So long as the preference changes themselves are regarded with indifference, there is no problem.

However, this need not be the case. It may happen that a person believes at one time that he will at some future time accept general evaluative principles—principles about what things *constitute* reasons for action—which he now finds pernicious. Moreover he may believe that in the future he will find his present values pernicious. What does prudence require of him in that case? Prudence requires that he take measures which promote the realization of that for which there *will* be reason. Do his beliefs at the earlier time give him any grounds for judging what he will have reason to do at the later? It is not clear to me that they do, and if not, then the requirement of prudence or timeless reasons may not be applicable.[1]

7. I have offered an abstract argument for timeless reasons which depends upon the integration of two standpoints, tensed and tenseless, from which an individual can regard his situation. Let me close this chapter with the suggestion that the original appearance of reasons for promoting the satisfaction of primary, unmotivated desires, and the fact that all reasons must admit of derivative application, can be better understood if they, too,

---

[1] On the other hand he *may* have a clear view about the matter. Suppose for example that he now believes that in twenty years he will value security, status, wealth, and tranquility, whereas now he values sex, spontaneity, frequent risks, and strong emotions. A decisive response to this situation could take either of two forms. The individual may be strongly enough convinced of the worthlessness of his inevitable future values simply to refuse them any claim on his present concern. He would then regard his present values as valid for the future also, and no prudential reasons would derive from his expected future views. On the other hand he may treat both his present and future values like preferences, regarding them each as sources of reasons under a higher principle: 'Live in the life-style of your choice.' That would demand of him a certain prudence about keeping open the paths to eventual respectability. In either case, his position would be formulable in terms of timeless reasons.

are connected with the conditions of personal unity. The point of this digression is to reinforce the claim that we must turn to metaphysics for explanation of the basic features of rational motivation.

Let us first consider how the natural desires give rise to reasons. A primary appetite begins as something which happens to the subject, and can occasionally be kept in that status, regarded as an intrusion or at any rate a peripheral curiosity. In that case one may be satisfied merely to keep it quiet, so that it does not interfere with pursuits that are more central.

But it is clear that someone who disregarded all his appetites or satisfied them only instrumentally, because if left unsatisfied they would interfere with his true goals, would be a radically dissociated individual. The type of dissociation which is important here is, I think, dissociation from the body. If someone uses his body only as an instrument for the pursuit of rationally accepted goals defined by reasons not stemming from the body itself and its desires, then it is as though another, more sensual person were residing in that body and being ignored by the rational subject who controlled it in deliberate action. Or, if not ignored, attended to only as a nuisance and a subject for repression.

To avoid such dissociation it is not necessary to incorporate every bodily impulse or inclination into the rational system. The principle of selection may be some type of centrality to the bodily life of the individual. Hunger, thirst, sexual desire, the impulse to general physical activity, the curiosity of the senses, all are fundamental to having a body in the sense not merely of having a body at one's *disposal*, but being, essentially, a physical person. The central emotions, too, fall into this category, although the higher on the intellectual scale one goes in the classification of impulses, the more susceptible they are to intellectual criticism.

Unity of the body, and of the person, also underlies the fact that all reasons apply derivatively to whatever will promote that to which they apply primarily. If I sign a cheque, it is not the act of my right hand, but my act; and there is more to me than my right hand. Suppose that I have a reason to write a cheque, but my right hand is holding a package. Since the reason is not the hand's, to write, but mine, to write with it, and since I have an extended and useful body at my disposal, this gives me reason to take the package in my left hand to free my right. Would it not be absurd to suggest that a further factor is required to make the connection—either to motivate such an act or to explain its rationality? What could the factor be? A further link is superfluous because nothing could link two hands more closely than the fact that they are both hands of the same person, and that an act engaging one of them is necessarily an act of the possessor of the other.

These examples show that the conception of oneself as a single individual plays an important *general* role in determining behaviour and the form of practical reasoning; not only through the connection between temporal unity and timeless reasons. And in all these cases, the appropriate behaviour will consequently be among the criteria for ascribing to an individual the relevant aspect of the conception.

PART THREE

OBJECTIVE REASONS AND ALTRUISM

IX

ALTRUISM: THE INTUITIVE ISSUE

1. The problem of how, if at all, altruism is possible has much in common with the corresponding problem about prudence. By altruism I mean not abject self-sacrifice, but merely a willingness to act in consideration of the interests of other persons, without the need of ulterior motives.[1] How is it possible that such considerations should motivate us at all? What sort of system, and what further intervening factors, are necessary in order to justify and to explain behaviour which has as its object the benefit of others? (As in the case of prudence, the problem can be treated without attempting to provide too fine an analysis of benefit and harm, happiness, unhappiness, pleasure, pain, or whatever the principal determinants, positive and negative, are to be. The question is not why these particular factors motivate, but how, given that they motivate in one way, they can also motivate in another—over time or across the gap between persons.)

The problem at this stage is not how the interests of others can motivate us to some specific policy of altruistic conduct, but how they can motivate us at all. Obviously *some* account of such behaviour is needed by most ethical theories, since there are few which do not include some requirements of other-regarding action. Even if the required social behaviour does not include serious self-sacrifice, it will almost certainly include cases in which no obviously self-interested motive is present, and in which some inconvenience or at least no benefit to the agent is likely to result. A defence of altruism in terms of self-interest is therefore unlikely to be successful. But there are other interests to which appeal may be made, including the indiscriminate general sentiments of sympathy or benevolence.

It is possible to argue against such hypotheses on the ground

---

[1] I shall put aside for the time being all questions about the relative weight to be assigned to the interests of oneself and others, in a system of reasons which can qualify as altruistic.

that the psychological and societal principles to which they appeal are neither universal nor obvious enough to account for the extent of altruistic motivation, and that they are evidently false to the phenomena.[1] However, I prefer to concentrate instead on trying to provide a better account, thereby showing that an appeal to our interests or sentiments, to account for altruism, is superfluous. My general reply to such suggestions is that without question people may be motivated by benevolence, sympathy, love, redirected self-interest, and various other influences, on some of the occasions on which they pursue the interests of others, but that there is also something else, a motivation available when none of those are, and also operative when they are present, which has genuinely the status of a rational requirement on human conduct. There is in other words such a thing as pure altruism (though it may never occur in isolation from all other motives). It is the direct influence of one person's interest on the actions of another, simply because in itself the interest of the former provides the latter with a reason to act. If any further internal factor can be said to interact with the external circumstances in such a case, it will be not a desire or an inclination but the structure represented by such a system of reasons.

A suggestion of this sort will have to deal with opposition similar to that evoked by the corresponding thesis about prudential motives. With regard to prudence, we had to contend with the intuition that since even when preparing for the future I am acting in the present, it must be a present reason which motivates me, something which I want now. With regard to altruism, the corresponding intuition is that since it is I who am acting, even when I act in the interests of another, it must be an interest of mine which provides the impulse. If so, any convincing

---

[1] There is one common account which can perhaps be disposed of here; the view that other-regarding behaviour is motivated by a desire to avoid the guilt feelings which would result from selfish behaviour. Guilt cannot provide the basic reason, because guilt is precisely the pained recognition that one is acting or has acted contrary to a reason which the claims, rights, or interests of others provide—a reason which must therefore be antecedently acknowledged.

Let me add that a similar argument can be given against appeals to a generalized sympathy as the basis of moral motivations. Sympathy is not, in general, just a feeling of discomfort produced by the recognition of distress in others, which in turn motivates one to relieve their distress. Rather, it is the pained awareness of their distress *as something to be relieved*.

justification of apparently altruistic behaviour must appeal to what *I* want.

The same prejudices are in operation here which have been observed to influence discussions of prudence: the conviction that every motivation must conform to the model of an inner force; the view that behind every motivated action lies a desire which provides the active energy for it; the assumption that to provide a justification capable also of *explaining* action, an appropriate motivation, usually a desire, must be among the conditions of the justification. If, as seems unavoidable, we are to explain the influence on a person of factors external to him in terms of their interaction with something internal to him, it is natural to assume that a desire, which can take the good of others directly or indirectly as its object, must provide the motivational force behind altruistic conduct. Bluntly: the belief that an act of mine will benefit someone else can motivate me only because I want his good, or else want something which involves it.[1]

The general assumptions behind such a view have been criticized at length in Chapter V, and I do not propose to repeat those criticisms here, for they apply without significant variation and with equal validity to the present employment of these assumptions. Briefly: in so far as a desire must be present if I am motivated to act in the interest of another, it need not be a desire of the sort which can form the *basis* for a motivation. It may, instead, be a desire which is itself motivated by reasons which the other person's interests provide. And if that is so, it cannot be among the conditions for the presence of such reasons. Desire is not the only possible source of motivation. Therefore we may look for other internal factors which connect belief and action in the altruistic case. Instead of ending the explanation with an altruistic desire which is simply postulated, we can do better by inquiring how such desires are possible, and what in our nature makes us capable of wanting other people's happiness or well-being.

---

[1] The bluntness of this position may be modified, however, by the observation that it permits a distinction between selfish and unselfish behaviour. If what I want is genuinely another's happiness, the object of my actions may simply *be* his happiness, rather than the satisfaction of my own desire for it. This point was made by Joseph Butler long ago, in opposition to the claim that all action is motivated by self-love; *Fifteen Sermons Preached at the Rolls Chapel* (London, 1726), esp. Sermon XI, 'Upon the Love of Our Neighbor'.

The account I offer will depend on a formal feature of practical reasoning which has a metaphysical explanation.

Alternative hypotheses fail as plausible candidates for a complete account of altruistic action because none of them provides the type of simple, absolute generality which is required. There is a considerateness for others which is beyond the reach of complicated reflections about social advantage, and which does not require the operation of any specific sentiment. The task is to discover an account of this general, passionless motivation which will make its existence plausible. Introspective and empirical investigation are not very useful in this area since the motivation is often partly or completely blocked in its operation by the interference of corrupting factors: repression, rationalization, blindness, weakness. Arguments and theoretical considerations can, however, reveal the form of an altruistic *component* in practical reason, which will be one contribution among others to the genesis of action.

2. The rational altruism which I shall defend can be intuitively represented by the familiar argument, 'How would you like it if someone did that to you?' It is an argument to which we are all in some degree susceptible; but how it works, how it can be persuasive, is a matter of controversy. We may assume that the situation in which it is offered is one in which you would not like it if another person did to you what you are doing to someone now (the formula can be changed depending on the type of case; it can probably be used, if it works at all, to persuade people to help others as well as to avoid hurting them). But what follows from this? If no one *is* doing it to you, how can your conduct be influenced by the hypothetical admission that if someone were, you would not like it?

Various hypotheses suggest themselves. It could be that you are afraid that your present behaviour will have the result that someone *will* do the same to you; your behaviour might bring this about either directly or through the encouragement of a general practice of some kind. It could be that the thought of yourself in a position similar to that of your victim is so vivid and unpleasant that you find it distasteful to go on persecuting the wretch. But what if you have neither this belief nor this degree of affective response? Or alternatively, why cannot such con-

siderations motivate you to increase your security against re-
taliation, or take a tranquillizer to quell your pity, rather than
to desist from your persecutions?

There is something else to the argument; it does not appeal
solely to the passions, but is a genuine argument whose conclusion is a judgment. The essential fact is that you would not
only *dislike* it if someone else treated you in that way; you would
resent it. That is, you would think that your plight gave the other
person a reason to terminate or modify his contribution to it,
and that in failing to do so he was acting contrary to reasons
which were plainly available to him. In other words, the argument appeals to a *judgment* that you would make in the hypothetical case, a judgment applying a general principle which is
relevant to the present case as well. It is a question not of com-
passion but of simply connecting, in order to see what one's
attitudes commit one to.

Recognition of the other person's reality, and the possibility
of putting yourself in his place, is essential. You see the present
situation as a specimen of a more general scheme, in which the
characters can be exchanged. The crucial factor injected into
this scheme is an attitude which you have towards your own
case, or rather an aspect of the view which you take of your own
needs, actions, and desires. You attribute to them, in fact, a
certain objective interest, and the recognition of others as persons like yourself permits extension of this objective interest to
the needs and desires of persons in general, or to those of any
particular individual whose situation is being considered. That
is accomplished by the schematic argument. But the initial intuition in your own case is what must be investigated.

It is important that the reasons which you believe others have
to consider your interests, should not refer to them specifically
as *yours*. That is, you must be prepared to grant that if you were
in the position in question, other people would have as their
reason to help you simply that *someone* was in need of help.
Otherwise there would be no way of concluding from the presence of such reasons in the event that you needed help to the
presence of similar reasons in the present case, when someone
else is in the unfortunate situation and you are in a position to
help him. So to explain how the argument works, we must discover an aspect of your attitude towards your own needs,

desires, and interests, which permits you to regard them as worthy of consideration simply as *someone's* needs, desires, and interests, rather than as yours.

If there actually is such an attitude, then the form of the intuitive argument we have been considering is not really essential—since it will be possible to bring that attitude to bear on the needs, desires and interests of another person directly. His interests are *someone's* interests as much as yours are. However, the argument at least reveals the connection between attitudes towards your own and towards other cases, and allows us to focus our analysis on attitudes of the former type, which are more vivid and require less imaginative effort. If one's sense of the reality of other persons is already sufficiently vivid, the argument may be superfluous; but since most of us are in varying degrees blind to other people, it is useful to be asked to imagine ourselves in their place, thus appealing to an objective element in the concern we feel for ourselves, and generalizing from that.

I shall therefore concentrate on each person's practical and evaluative judgments about his own needs, etc.; especially the relation between the reasons they give him to act because they are *his* needs, and the reasons he thinks they provide for others to act, simply because they are *someone's* needs. Our primary task will be to discover a foundation for the latter belief.

3. The primary opposition to my view comes from egoism, a general position which corresponds in this controversy to the preference of dated to timeless reasons in the controversy over prudence. Egoism holds that each individual's reasons for acting and possible motivations for acting, must arise from his own interests and desires, however those interests may be defined. The interests of one person can on this view motivate another or provide him with a reason only if they are connected with his interests or are objects of some sentiment of his, like sympathy, pity, or benevolence.

Those who occupy this philosophical position may believe that they are, as a matter of psychological fact, egoists, but I doubt that there are any genuine specimens of the type. It should be noticed how peculiar egoism would be in practice; it would have to show itself not only in the lack of a direct concern for others but also in an inability to regard one's own concerns as being of interest to anyone else, except instrumentally or contingently upon the operation of some sentiment. An egoist who needs help, before concluding that anyone else has reason to assist him, must be able to answer the question 'What's it to him?' He is precluded from feeling resentment, which embodies the judgment that another is failing to act on reasons with which one's own needs provide him. No matter how extreme his own concern the egoist will not feel that this in itself need be of interest to anyone else. The pain which gives him a reason to remove his gouty toes from under another person's heel does not in itself give the other any reason to remove the heel, since it is not his pain.

Anyone who thinks he is an egoist should imagine himself in either role in such a situation. Can he truly affirm that the owner of the heel has no reason whatever to remove it from the gouty toes? Particularly if one owns the toes, it shows a rare detachment not to regard the pain as simply in itself a bad thing, which there is reason for anyone to avert. It is difficult, in other words, to resist the tendency to objectify the negative value which one assigns to pain, or would assign to it if one experienced it, regarding the identity of its owner as irrelevant.

The procedure may be different for different kinds of reasons, but the idea is the same: that in accepting goals or reasons myself I attach objective value to certain circumstances, not just value for myself; similarly when I acknowledge that others have reason to act in their own interests, these must finally be reasons not just for them, but objective reasons for the goals which they pursue or the acts which they perform.

Arguments against the coherency of ethical egoism have been offered in the past, and it may be in order to distinguish them from the one I propose to offer. The arguments with which I am familiar all focus on egoism as a universal position, and find incoherencies in the judgments which it requires a man to make about other people, and in what it requires him in general to urge or support. I wish to suggest, on the other hand, that ethical egoism is already objectionable in its application by each person to his *own* case, and to his own reasons for action. Let me mention briefly some earlier arguments.

There is the position of G. E. Moore, who claimed that

egoism involves a straightforward contradiction, for it asserts 'that *each* man's happiness is the sole good—that a number of different things are *each* of them the only good thing there is—an absolute contradiction!' An egoist may be inclined to object that his view is only that each man's happiness or interest is the sole good *for him* but Moore has already disallowed this move:

> When I talk of a thing as 'my own good', all that I can mean is that something which will be exclusively mine (whatever be the various senses of this relation denoted by 'possession'), is also *good absolutely;* or rather that my possession of it is *good absolutely.* The *good* of it can in no possible sense be 'private' or belong to me; any more than a thing can *exist* privately, or *for* one person only. The only reason I can have for aiming at 'my own good', is that it is *good absolutely* that what I so call should belong to me—*good absolutely* that I should *have* something, which, if I have it, others cannot have. But if it is *good absolutely* that I should have it, then everyone else has as much reason for aiming at *my* having it, as I have myself.[1]

He goes on to say more to the same effect, but nothing resembling an argument is offered for these claims.[2] What I wish to explain is exactly what he assumes: that in order to accept something as a goal for oneself, one must be able to regard its achievement by oneself as an *objective* good.

Other arguments, such as those of Medlin[3] and Baier,[4] point out that egoism leads to inconsistent attitudes and behaviour if, as an ethical doctrine, it is to govern not only one's own actions but also what one wants and encourages others to do, or what one is obliged to permit them to do. But if these objections are

[1] *Principia Ethica* (Cambridge, 1903), p. 99. Although Moore treats egoism as a theory about the good, while I treat it as a theory about reasons, the two are clearly related, since Moore believes that the good is that at which one has reason to aim. I myself do not wish to make any claims about good and bad, or about their relation to reasons for action.

[2] They seem to him self-evident because he regards it as already established that 'good' is a one-place predicate denoting a simple, non-natural property. But that would not be granted by an egoist, whose fundamental evaluative concept would be a *relation*: 'X is good for Y.' A similar criticism is made by C. D. Broad, 'Certain Features in Moore's Ethical Doctrines', in *The Philosophy of G. E. Moore*, ed. P. A. Schilpp (Evanston and Chicago, 1942).

[3] Brian Medlin, 'Ultimate Principles and Ethical Egoism', *Australasian Journal of Philosophy* (1957).

[4] Kurt Baier, *The Moral Point of View* (Ithaca: Cornell University Press, 1958); abridged edition (New York: Random House, 1965), p. 95.

correct, they leave a more fundamental question unanswered: Why should the acceptance of a universal principle of conduct commit one to any desires at all about the conformity of others to that principle? Why should the judgment that another person has reason to act in certain ways provide you with *any* reason for wanting him to do so?

There is a further question: Why need one adopt *general* principles of action at all—i.e. principles applying to others besides oneself? Why can one not restrict oneself to the acceptance of personal principles of action—which may be construed as intentions, some longer-term or more general than others but all nevertheless applicable only to one's own behaviour? About this question something will be said later on.

It is a requirement of universality on practical principles, in a specific form which excludes most types of egoism, that will be defended here. And it will be supported by reflections about what happens when one acts in one's own interest. That case by itself contains the basis for a challenge to egoism.

It should be emphasized that by 'egoism' I mean the relatively narrow and specific view that the only source of reasons for action lies in the interests of the agent. The term might also be applied to a variety of other views, and I do not propose to argue against all of them. Some fall prey to the general argument which will be offered; others do not. And of the latter, some (e.g. egoism as an instrumental policy likely to lead to everyone's happiness if generally practised) can be refuted on empirical grounds,[1] whereas others perhaps cannot (e.g. the view that life is like a competitive game, which it is objectively good that everyone should play to win). More will be said on this subject in the course of the argument.

4. I shall attempt to explain altruism, like prudence, as a rational requirement on action. Just as it became clear in the earlier discussion that prudence is not fundamental, but derives from the requirement that reasons be timelessly formulable, so it will turn out that altruism is not fundamental, but derives from

---

[1] On the other hand, if an instrumental egoism should be supported by *true* empirical premises, it need not conflict with altruism. If in fact egoistic conduct is the best means to the general happiness, then altruism probably requires it. But that is not the egoism that I am talking about.

something more general: a formal principle which can be specified without mentioning the interests of others at all. That principle will, moreover, be closely analogous to the formal principle of timelessness, in that it will deny the possibility of restricting to one *person* the derivative influence of a reason for action, just as the formal principle which underlies prudence denies the possibility of restricting such derivative influence to one *time*. The principle underlying altruism will require, in other words, that all reasons be construable as expressing objective rather than subjective values. In both cases the relevant condition on reasons is a purely formal one, compatible with considerable variety in the content of those reasons which satisfy it. Therefore the acceptance of prudence, or of altruism, is no substitute for a general theory of value and human interests. Both prudence and altruism impose conditions on the derivative influence of primary reasons whose sources lie elsewhere.

The attempt to discover such a general requirement on conduct as I have described, and to provide a plausible interpretation of it, is indebted to the earlier efforts to defend prudence. Not only the general enterprise, but also the form of the present principle and the method of interpretation will parallel those of the earlier case. Specifically, it will be argued that the condition of *objectivity* (as I shall call it) is the practical expression of a conception possessed by any rational, acting subject, though not in this case the conception of himself as temporally extended. As has been indicated in Ch. IV, §1, the conception underlying altruism is that of oneself as merely one person among others, and of others as persons in just as full a sense. This is parallel to the central element in a conception of oneself as temporally extended: that the present is just a time among others, and that other times are equally real. As we shall see, the two views have similar analyses and parallel consequences.

My argument is intended to demonstrate that altruism (or its parent principle) depends on a full recognition of the reality of other persons. Nevertheless the central conception in my proposed interpretation will be a conception of *oneself*, and the argument will rest on an analysis of how this conception bears on self-interested action. This method is allowable, because recognition of the reality of others depends on a conception of oneself, just as recognition of the reality of the future depends on a conception of the present.[1]

The precise form of altruism which derives from this argument will depend on a further factor, namely the nature of the primary reasons for action which individuals possess. If these are tied to the pursuit of their interests, in some ordinary sense of that term, then a normal requirement of altruism will be the result. But if the general reasons with which we begin are not tied to individual goals, the resulting objective system may require the common pursuit of certain goals without involving altruism in the usual sense at all, i.e. concern for the needs and interests of other individuals.

It is not at all obvious what our interests are, let alone what part they play in determining reasons for our conduct. I doubt, for one thing, that the satisfaction of basic desires comes anywhere near to exhausting the notion of interest. Moreover, there may be values which have nothing to do with interests at all. I do not in fact possess a general theory of the values to be embodied in a catalogue of primary reasons, but I am fairly certain that they are complicated enough to ensure that even if the formal result defended here is correct, what will emerge from it is neither utilitarianism, nor any other moral system which is simply altruistic. More will be said about this later.

[1] In fact, since altruism is in a sense a hypothetical principle, stating what one has reason to do *if* what one does will affect the interests of others, it could be accepted even by someone who believed that there were no other people. Without believing in their actual existence, he could still believe in the reality of other persons in the sense that he might regard himself as a type of individual of which there could be other specimens, as real as he was. The source of this hypothetical altruism towards these possible other beings would lie in the connection between the conception of himself which allowed him to believe in their possibility, and his own self-interested concerns.

X

OBJECTIVE REASONS

1. The principle behind altruism is that values must be objective, and that any which appear subjective must be associated with others that are not. In any situation in which there is reason for one person to promote some end, we must be able to discover an end which there is reason for anyone to promote, should he be in a position to do so. The explication and defence of this thesis will require the introduction of a formal distinction between subjective and objective reasons.

It was said in Ch. VII, §1 that every reason can be expressed by a predicate R, such that for all persons p and events A, if R is true of A, then p has prima facie reason to promote A. This is the basic formula for the specification of a general reason. I shall not repeat here all the earlier qualifications and explanations of its terms, except to note that the predicate R may, or may not, contain a free occurrence of the variable p, and that if it does, this is to be referred to as a free agent-variable. It is assumed, then, that reasons are universal—i.e. in some sense the same for all persons—and that they transmit their influence to actions suitably related to ends to which they apply. The issue now is whether, if a reason at the highest level of generality applies to something, that is something which *anyone* has reason to promote.

This issue arises even after the universality of reasons over persons is admitted, for universal reasons can be defined which yield distinct but related ends of action for different individuals. We may describe such reasons as subjective. Formally, a subjective reason is one whose defining predicate R contains a free occurrence of the variable p. (The free agent-variable will, of course, be free only *within R*; it will be bound by the universal quantification over persons which governs the entire formula.) All universal reasons and principles expressible in terms of the basic formula either contain a free agent-variable or they do not. The former are subjective; the latter will be called objective.

Some examples will be helpful. Suppose G. E. Moore finds

himself in the path of an oncoming truck, and concludes that he has reason to remove himself. The bare condition that reasons must be universal requires that he be able to formulate the reason in general terms. If he is asked *what* reason he has to get out of the way, he may say (among other things) any of the following:

(a) that the act will prolong G. E. Moore's life;
(b) that the act will prolong his life;
(c) that the act will prolong someone's life.

Each of these might be alleged to be a general reason, valid for all persons. Reason (b), however, is a subjective one, for the word 'his' is a free agent-variable. The full representation of the reason would be: 'Everyone has reason to do what will prolong *his* life.' Or, more formally,

(b) (p,A) (If A will prolong p's life, then p has reason to promote A).[1]

(It will be recalled that in the limiting case, if A is an action, doing A is to count as promoting A.)

(a) and (c), on the other hand, are objective reasons, for they contain no open reference to the doer of any act to which they may be applied.[2] Consequently, they are not just universal reasons in the sense that anyone can have them; they are in addition reasons for anyone to promote what they apply to. They are not reasons *for* particular individuals, but simply reasons for the *occurrence* of the things of which they hold true. (This last formulation may be unacceptable to some. For the purpose of my argument, however, it is not necessary to distinguish between objective reasons as reasons for things simply to occur, and as reasons for *anyone* to want and promote those things to which they apply.)

---

[1] I shall employ the unanalysed notion of 'prolonging one's life' for convenience, although a more precise concept can certainly be formulated and would probably provide a more exact statement of the reason which is operative in these cases. What is desirable, fundamentally, is *being* alive over the succeeding time, the more of it the better.

[2] Formally, they may be expressed as follows:
   (a) (p, A) (If A will prolong Moore's life, then p has reason to promote A.)
   (c) (p, A) (If (∃q) (A will prolong q's life), then p has reason to promote A.)
In the latter case the reason is objective not because R contains no variable ranging over persons, but because the variable is bound in R, and hence is not a free agent-variable; (R(A) being in this case (∃q) (A will prolong q's life)).

2. The distinction can be more thoroughly understood if it is applied to problematic cases. Consider for example the following possible reply to a request for Moore's reason for getting out of the way:

(d) That the act is one which will prolong the life of its agent.

Is this a subjective or an objective reason? That depends on how one reads it. If it is taken to be equivalent to (b), it is of course subjective. But there is another way of taking it, according to which it provides a reason for anyone to promote an act which will prolong the life of its agent—whether or not that agent is himself.[1] On that reading, the reason is objective. In its primary application it overlaps significantly with the subjective version; i.e. the two reasons apply to many of the same acts, acts by which individuals prolong their own lives. But the derivative influence of the objective reason extends also to acts which promote the occurrence of acts by *others* which will prolong *their* lives. It represents a curious value: the objective value of self-reliance in matters of basic survival and self-preservation. Perhaps no one would offer this particular reason for getting out of the way of a truck. Nevertheless reasons of this *type* are quite important: namely, those which assign objective value to a certain kind of behaviour, rather than to any goal of that behaviour. Such reasons apply both to the behaviour itself and to what will promote it, whether in oneself or in others. They will play a significant role in any system of objective principles; consequently a more exact account of their operation is in order.

Observe that the behaviour to which these reasons assign objective value may be precisely the behaviour indicated by certain subjective reasons. Given any subjective principle, one can construct a corresponding objective principle which accords primary objective value to acts of the sort justified by the subjective one. Consider, for example, the following principles, which are ambiguous between subjective and objective:

[1] Formally:

(p, A) (If A is an act which will prolong the life of its agent, then p has reason to promote A.)

Note that R contains no free agent-variable, for R(A) is 'A is an act which will prolong the life of its agent', or $(\exists q)$ (A will prolong q's life and A is an act of q). This contains only the *bound* person variable, q. Of course the reason applies in the case when p and q are the same person.

(e) Everyone should improve his mind;
(f) Everyone should help his family;
(g) Everyone should defend his country.[1]

All three principles contain the word 'his', which will yield a subjective reason if it is construed as a free agent-variable. In that case each person, for example, has reason to improve his mind, and to do what will enable him to improve it, but whether he improves it or not is of no concern to anyone else, because the free agent-variable prevents the transmission of derivative influence to any acts of another person. Other people have only their own minds to worry about. I shall not bother to provide formal statements of these subjective principles; their nature should be clear. Each of the three subjective reasons systematically assigns to things values *for* people; for each person, *his* mind, *his* family, *his* country is a rational object of concern. But nothing is implied about other minds, other families, other countries—or even about the objective value of his own.

On the other hand the principles can also be construed objectively; i.e. as assigning *objective* value to the pursuit of mental self-improvement, support of one's family, or defence of one's country. The reasons then apply in the first instance to conduct which meets these descriptions, but they also apply, derivatively, to actions which promote more conduct of the same kind, whether in oneself or in others. Two things must be noticed: first, that no objective value is assigned by such a principle as it stands to the *goals* of the specified behaviour: good minds, well-off families, secure countries. These goals may be accepted independently—and probably would be acknowledged by anyone accepting the three objective principles; but they are not entailed by those principles. The objective version of (g), for example, does not require me to defend anyone else's country.

Second, such reasons permit a very obvious distinction between primary and secondary applications. Reason (g), for example, can apply primarily only to acts of the person whose country is concerned. Its only application to the acts of others will be a derivative one, and this may bear significantly on the strength of the reasons so produced. Suppose that one man forms a guerrilla band to harry a foreign army which is invading his

---

[1] I am here concerned only with the form of these principles, not with their truth.

country, and another man supplies him with arms. It makes a difference whether the second man is from the same country as the first. If he is, then his action falls not only under the derivative influence of objective reason (g) but also under its direct application. If he is from a different country, the reason will apply only derivatively (unless the defence of the former country is essential to the defence of the latter), and probably with less force. If he is from the same country as the invading army, his provision of arms to the enemy falls under the same reason directly, but in a contrary sense; against rather than for—and probably the direct application will have priority over the indirect when they conflict, on any plausibly elaborated version of such a system of values.

This case is worth pursuing further, just to make the subjective–objective distinction clear. Suppose we try to construct an objective principle which yields reasons for all and only the same acts as the subjective version of (g). I maintain that it cannot be done. Clearly the objective version of (g) is not good enough, but suppose we try to supplement it with a further principle which cancels its excess implications. For example, it may be held that everyone should defend his country and not contribute to the defence of another country unless in so doing he also contributes to the defence of his own, or unless there is some independent reason for doing so, having nothing to do with defence. This will admittedly cut out reasons for assisting foreigners to defend their countries. But if conduct of this sort is regarded as having objective value, the principle will encourage acts likely to produce such conduct in *general* whether it be the conduct of one's fellow countrymen or of foreigners. Thus, first of all, there will be prima facie reason at least not to interfere with another's efforts in this direction, so long as they do not threaten one's *own* country. And second, one would have reason to discourage foreigners from coming to the assistance of countries other than their own, unless it should be one's own country, in which case the primary duty of patriotism might take precedence.

In short, no matter how complicated one makes the defining predicate R, so long as it remains objective, the derivative influence of the reason will eventually extend beyond the range covered by any related subjective reason; one will have reason at least to encourage or allow others to do likewise, to some extent. This is important, for it is a condition of the significance of my position that it is not possible systematically to produce an objective principle which will yield all and only the same consequences as a given subjective one. Any objective principle or reason which yields all the consequences of a given subjective one will yield others in addition.

3. The distinction between subjective and objective reasons cuts across various others. In fact, it appears likely that most things—pleasure, knowledge, art, patriotism, etc.—could be assigned values which were either subjective or objective. Subjective and objective value are not the values of different kinds of things, but rather formally different kinds of value each of which it is in general intelligible to assign to the same kind of thing. Anything may be said to have value simply, or only *for* someone to whom it stands in a certain relation (but for the latter to be a subjective value, it cannot be the case that the person's *possession* or *achievement* of the object has value simply, given the appropriate relation between him and it).[1]

Moreover, objective reasons can yield different goals for different individuals, and subjective reasons may yield common goals for all individuals. The former point is obvious, for different individuals, depending on their circumstances, will have reason to do different things in the service of a single objectively valuable end. Therefore what they have reason to do, and the major subsidiary goals they have reason to pursue, may vary greatly. The second point is less obvious but more important, particularly in connection with ethics. Subjective reasons hold for everyone, but assign in the first instance a different but related goal to each person: *his* happiness, *his* security, the welfare of *his* family or *his* country. However, for a given subjective reason there may be certain circumstances which realize the relevant goal for everyone. Hobbes's ethical doctrine depends

---

[1] One reason the distinction is easily lost sight of is this: just as there is an ambiguity in 'p has reason to do A at t', regarding the function of the time index (for it may mean either 'p has at t a reason to do A' or 'p has a reason to (do A at t))—so there is an ambiguity in regard to the person index when we say, 'There is reason for p to do A.' It may mean either 'There is (for p) reason to do A' or 'There is reason for (p to do A).' In the latter case the value, or reason, has no person-index and is not a value *for* anyone. In the former case, the reason is truly subjective.

on the assumption that a stable, well-policed society will be overwhelmingly in the interest of each of its members, so that a mere consideration of his own individual interest provides each with a reason to pursue and preserve that condition. Nevertheless, this is different from the case in which social order, or the general welfare, is regarded as objectively valuable—something which everyone has an original reason to promote, rather than a reason derivative from his own personal stake in it.

Not all subjective reasons are egoistic, as can be seen from the subjective versions of examples (f) and (g) above. Some subjective principles may require extreme self-sacrifice in the service of subjectively defined ends.[1] Moreover, not all objective principles are altruistic. Some may dictate pursuit of a goal which involves *no one's* interest, rather than the interests of either oneself or others; for example a retributive theory of punishment, which counts punishment a good thing aside from its benefit to the criminal, to his victim, or to society. Some objective principles can even be quasi-egoistic, in the sense that they primarily encourage self-interested behaviour—as can be seen from example (d) and the objective version of (e).

Nevertheless, the central version of egoism is a subjective one. The most philosophically attractive view (and hence the one most worth refuting) is one which denies that reasons depend on the assignment of objective value to anything, and which finds egoism acceptable because it requires only subjective values. It must be emphasized that such an egoist cannot even assign objective value to the circumstance in which everyone behaves in accordance with his favoured principle, for that would immediately let in objective, non-egoistic reasons to promote that desirable state of affairs, and he would no longer be a pure egoist.

4. The thesis which I propose to defend is simply that the only acceptable reasons are objective ones; even if one operates successfully with a subjective principle, one must be able to back it up with an objective principle yielding those same reasons as well as (presumably) others. Whenever one acts for a reason, I maintain, it must be *possible* to regard oneself as acting for an objective

---

[1] C. D. Broad has coined the expression 'Self-referential Altruism' to describe such views (see Broad. op. cit.).

reason, and promoting an objectively valuable end. Since
the variety of types of objective reason is considerable—they
may assign value either to ends of action or to actions themselves,
for example—there are various possible ways of providing objective rational backing for a given course of action. Eventually
we shall have to distinguish between these possibilities, but for
the moment let us consider the general thesis that all reasons
must be derivable from objective principles.

In view of all the qualifications entered so far, it may seem
reckless to characterize this as an attack on egoism and a defence of altruism. After all, there are many possible objective
principles unconnected with altruism, and an argument merely
to the effect that reasons must be objective provides us with no
way of choosing among the candidates. Some of them, indeed,
may encourage self-serving behaviour, notably (d) or a suitably
expanded version thereof. Any objective principle which demands self-reliance, self-defence, or self-improvement will not be
altruistic, although it will encourage a different kind of concern
about others. Moreover, not all the principles excluded by an
argument against subjective reasons will be egoistic. Certainly
pure egoism is only one subjective principle among many. (An
extreme case of a subjective principle would be that everyone
should act *only* in the interest of others, and never in his own
interest; 'pure' self-abnegating altruism, in other words.)

For all these reasons additional premises are necessary to
reach substantive conclusions from the result that practical
reasons must be objective. One needs something like a theory of
value. Nevertheless the formal result is significant, because there
are numerous things on whose value people are in rough general
agreement: pain, frustration, and coercion are bad; pleasure,
satisfaction, and freedom are good, by and large. In any case the
requirement of objectivity can be regarded as a condition on
whatever values one holds, and in fact I would support it in that
form regardless of its consequences for egoism and altruism.

But since it is widely believed that human interests and happiness have value as ends, an argument which shows that such
value must be conceived as objective will be in effect an argument for altruism, since it will mean that the ends are common
rational objects of pursuit for everyone. More complicated alternative objective principles are available and will have to be

examined, but it seems desirable to indicate in advance what relation the formal issue has to the substantive dispute between egoism and altruism, and in what sense I take myself to be arguing against the former and for the latter by arguing that all reasons must be ultimately specifiable in objective form.

Having said this, we may lay it aside until the formal thesis has been defended, after which it will be appropriate to take up the question of substantive practical consequences. Here again there is a parallel to the earlier discussion of prudence, where the issue was first reduced to a formal one, and after that had been discussed, separate consideration was given to the type of substantive prudential requirement that might be expected to follow from a system of timeless reasons.

XI

SOLIPSISM, DISSOCIATION, AND THE IMPERSONAL STANDPOINT

1. I have said that interpretation of the system of objective reasons on which altruism depends is parallel to the interpretation already proposed for the system of timeless reasons on which the possibility of prudence depends. Each interpretation relies on a distinct conception that every person has of himself, a conception displayed in his acceptance of the relevant type of reason.

The most general characterization of an interpretation is that it provides a metaphysical account of how a certain type of motivation is possible—not a *motivational* explanation in terms of desires, reasons, and so forth, but a description of certain structural conditions to which reasons must conform, and an account of what in the nature of human beings the presence of that structure depends on. The interpretation of prudence relates it to the conception of oneself as a temporally persistent being. The failure to accept as reasons for present action the reasons which one expects for the future, is the practical expression of a failure to identify with the temporally persistent person of whom one's present self is only a stage among others.

The validation of objective reasons must deal with a transmission of the influence of reasons from one person to another, corresponding to the transmission of their influence over time, and this may suggest that if the interpretations are to be parallel, the interpretation of altruism will have to link it to a mystical identification of oneself with other persons, or perhaps with a mass self consisting of all persons. But we have already seen why this is not necessary. To identify with one's future self is not to hold the absurd view that present and future stages of one's life are identical. One need only identify the present as one time among others all of which are contained in a single life. And what corresponds to this in the interpersonal case is not an identification of oneself with other persons or with all persons, but rather a conception of oneself as simply a person among others all of whom are included in a single world. Just as the crucial conception for the earlier argument had to do with the present, so the crucial conception for the present argument has to do with oneself. To recognize others fully as persons requires a conception of oneself as identical with a particular, impersonally specifiable inhabitant of the world, among others of a similar nature. Just as the earlier argument required a conception of the present not merely as *now*, but as a particular time, so the present argument requires a conception of oneself not merely as *I*, but as someone.

It was argued that only practical principles formulated in terms of timeless reasons could retain their motivational content for someone regarding the present as merely a time among others, all tenselessly describable. I shall argue here that only objective reasons permit the motivational content of practical judgments to be retained when those judgments are brought into accord with the impersonal conception of oneself as merely *someone*. Objective reasons retain their motivational content from this standpoint because they do not represent values *for* particular agents, but are rather reasons for things to occur or obtain, simply.

The essential parallel between the two arguments is that each relies on a distinction between two standpoints towards the world and oneself—one expressed with the aid of token-reflexives and the other not. The latter standpoint is temporal neutrality in the argument for prudence, impersonality in the argument for altruism; and it is those standpoints which require timelessness and objectivity, respectively, in the reasons for action which they are able to accommodate. Ethics is a struggle against a certain form of the egocentric predicament, just as prudential reasoning is a struggle against domination by the present.

2. The standpoint which contrasts with the impersonal I shall call the personal. We must now define them both, explain the relation between them, and describe their connection with solipsism and its denial.

The personal standpoint is often expressed by means of the grammatical first person, but it need not be. Other token-reflexives which pick out the subject and locate him with respect to what is being discussed, can also express the personal standpoint. The essence of personal judgments, beliefs, attitudes, etc., is that they view the world from a vantage point within it, and their subject or author is the locus of that vantage point. The impersonal standpoint, on the other hand, provides a view of the world without giving one's location in it. Descriptions from this standpoint do not require the first person or other token-reflexives. A complete impersonal description of the world will include a description of the person who is 'I' in the personal description, and will recast in impersonal terms everything that can be said about that individual in the first person. Thus the impersonal standpoint should be able to accommodate all phenomena describable from the personal standpoint, including facts about the subject himself.

The impersonal standpoint plays a role in the explication of the idea that one is just a person among others, much like the role played by tenseless statements in an account of what it is to regard the present as just a time among others. This emerges if we ask what it is to regard others as persons in fully the same sense in which one is a person oneself. First, one must have a conception of persons which permits this.

That means that it must be possible to say of other persons anything which one can say of oneself, and in the same sense. The assertion need not be true, but it must be significant. Shifts of grammatical person, like shifts of tense, cannot be permitted to alter the sense of what is asserted about the circumstance which is the subject of the statement. They represent only shifts in the point of view from which the observation is being offered. So any type of thing which one can significantly assert of oneself—what one is thinking, feeling, or doing—must be significantly ascribable in the same sense to others, whether by themselves in the first person or by persons other than themselves, in the second or third person. If I say of another individual that he is amused, there must be something in what I am saying about him that is identical with what I say of myself in saying 'I am amused'; or again, with what he can say of himself by making that same remark. Whether the case is one's own or another's, the same fact may be expressed from several points of view, using different grammatical persons; and although these statements will differ in certain of their implications, they also assert something in common. It is that common element which is singled out by the impersonal standpoint. The impersonal standpoint, like the standpoint of temporal neutrality, abstracts from the relation between the speaker and what is being spoken about, and merely asserts what can be asserted given *any* such relation.

I do not wish to minimize the importance of these relations. What is said or expressed when I say 'I am angry' may be very different from what is said or expressed on the same occasion by someone else, remarking of me, 'He is angry'. The bare distinction between myself and him, which justifies the grammatical change of person, is only one difference. Because of that difference innumerable others follow, having to do with the grounds for the assertion, the effect that can be produced by making it, and so forth. But all this should not obscure the fact that different persons (like different tenses) of the same statement can be employed from appropriately different standpoints to say something common about a given situation.

3. To regard oneself in every respect as merely a person among others, one must be able to regard oneself in every respect impersonally. I therefore propose the following principle. Whoever makes any judgment from the personal standpoint, whether about himself or about others, or not about anyone at all, is committed to two further judgments: (a) an impersonal judgment to the same effect about the same situation and characters; (b) a basic personal statement saying who, in the impersonally described scene, he is. The latter will justify the token-reflexives employed in the original judgment. This is not offered as an analysis of the personal judgment, or as a report of what thoughts are usually associated with it. I maintain only that one is committed by a personal judgment to the acceptance of such beliefs, if one regards oneself as merely a person among others.

Now it is of course true that distinct personal standpoints towards the same circumstance yield judgments and expectations that are extremely different. Given a situation with several characters in it, even if I know what it is like from the impersonal standpoint, I cannot know what to expect unless I also know my location in it. Just as I cannot know what form the evidence of a fire will take unless I know whether the fire is past, present, or future, so I cannot know what to expect in the way of evidence that one of the persons in a group has been poisoned unless I know whether it is I or someone else. And it seems likely that with certain psychological attributions, the difference between other standpoints and the first person will make the difference between needing evidence and needing none.

But every one of these differences between standpoints is itself the result of connections, principles and regularities which can be comprehended within the scope of the impersonal standpoint. All of the persons in a situation, and all of the viewpoints, expectations, and conditions of evidence associated with them, fall within a single impersonal conception. This will include impersonal specification of those relations between psychological states and behaviour (whatever they may be) which permit the ascription of psychological states on behavioural evidence. It will also include an impersonal statement of conditions on first-person psychological ascriptions, including the provision that some of them do not call for behavioural or observational evidence. Even the respects in which one's own experiences may be systematically different from those of others are open to impersonal description, for if one is just a person among others, one can be singled out impersonally, idiosyncrasies and all.

The only personal residue, therefore, which is not included in the system of impersonal beliefs to which I am committed by a personal judgment, is the basic personal premise itself, the premise which locates me in the world which has been impersonally described. The addition of this premise makes a great difference in *how* that world is conceived, but no difference in *what* is conceived to be the case. I can conceive impersonally my house burning down, and the individual T.N. standing before it, feeling hot and miserable, and looking hot and miserable to bystanders, and seeing their sympathetic looks, etc. etc. If I add to all this the premise that I am T.N., I will imagine *feeling* hot and miserable, *seeing* the sympathetic bystanders, etc.; but this is not to imagine anything happening differently. Anything which I can imagine feeling, I can imagine being felt by the person impersonally described, who I in fact am. Anything I can judge or believe about my own situation, experiences, actions, I can judge or believe about him, without any alteration in what is being believed to occur.

4. The above claims are not uncontroversial, for they are in opposition to solipsism, a view which has appeared in various attractive incarnations. It is not universally granted, for example, that first- and third-person psychological ascriptions have the same sense, or assert something in common. This is partly because they differ so radically in the grounds on which they are applied, and in the consequences, expectations, and activities associated with them. It has been suggested that the third-person claims may have a behaviouristic meaning, while the corresponding first-person claim merely *expresses* the psychological condition which it appears to report.

But the deep source for such a bifurcation of meaning comes from solipsism, and the view that what is meant by a first-person psychological ascription *cannot* be said of someone else. The connection is as follows. Solipsism, as a metaphysical rather than an epistemological position, denies sense to the supposition that there are other persons besides oneself.[1] It denies sense to that supposition on the ground that the concepts which one applies to one's own experiences do not include the possibility of application in the same sense to anything which is *not* one's experience. Moreover, this is thought not to be an accidental feature of the concepts one *possesses*; rather it is thought that any concepts which could apply univocally both to oneself and to what was not oneself would necessarily fail to be concepts which applied to one's own experiences.

In the *Blue Book*[2] Wittgenstein represents the solipsist as asking: 'If what I feel is always *my* pain only, what can the supposition mean that someone else feels pain?' This is a general problem about experience; pain serves only as an example. The solipsist's view is that the idea of pain is the idea of something *felt*, or experienced, a conception which comes from his own

---

[1] I suspect that the epistemological version of solipsism, namely that we can never know or even have evidence of the existence of other minds, is ultimately dependent on the metaphysical version; but we need not take that up here.

[2] *The Blue and Brown Books* (Oxford: Blackwell, 1958), p. 56.

experience. 'Pain is something like *this*,' he might say, concentrating on his arthritis, 'and how can anything which is not experienced by me be *this* sort of occurrence?' The reply that it might be experienced by someone else is of no help with *that* problem: for it presupposes an understanding of what it would be for the same thing to be experienced not by him but by another, and that understanding is exactly what is lacking. His view is that pain, something with which he is familiar, cannot be conceived apart from its relation to his own consciousness. A solipsist may retain the full range of first- and third-person psychological language, but he must regard himself as using it in a different sense (perhaps a behaviourist one) when he ascribes 'experiences' to 'others', from that which is operative when he describes his own experiences.

The connection of solipsism with the distinction between the personal and impersonal standpoints is fairly clear. According to the solipsist, an impersonal description of the situation in which he finds himself, and of his condition, cannot avoid being radically incomplete. It is incomplete not only because it fails to specify who he is, but because it fails to describe what is really happening. He might put it as follows: 'I know perfectly well what it is like for *someone* to have a headache, and I can tell when it is true, from his behaviour, etc.; but if it's *me*, then *this* is what happens.' (And here he would imagine *having* a headache.) 'That is a quite different type of occurrence, an inner occurrence, not at all like just *someone's* having a headache.'

In saying this a solipsist must be careful not to rely on ordinary psychological terms to specify what happens when *he* has a headache; for those terms—terms like 'dull, throbbing pain'—can apply to the experience of other persons, and also to his own, impersonally conceived. They do not therefore pick out the special occurrence of *his* having, e.g., a dull, throbbing pain. A solipsist must therefore have a system of personal conversion principles, as it were, which specify what someone's having a headache is like when it is *he* who has it, and so on for every other variety of psychological condition, connecting the impersonally ascribable state with what *his having it* is like. These can be regarded as the rules of a private language, or of the private component of the solipsist's language. (Actually his language and thought will be permeated with this private aspect, for it will enter in at every point of contact between language and his experience, whether he is talking about experience directly or only about other things, from a personal standpoint.[1])

This is not the place for an independent discussion of solipsism. I regard it as a position to be taken seriously; what is correct in it, I believe, is that if one begins with the sole idea of oneself and one's own experiences as a model, one may not have sufficient material to extrapolate to a significant notion of other selves and their experiences. I shall not argue for this view. If it is correct, then the avoidance of solipsism requires that the *conception* of other persons like oneself (not necessarily the belief that there are any) be included in the idea of one's own experiences from the beginning. This is achieved by a conception which permits every feature of one's own situation and experience to be described and regarded, without loss of content, from the impersonal standpoint. If that can be shown to be a general condition of the idea of one's own experiences, then there will be no chasm between that idea and the idea of other persons, and hence no insurmountable difficulty in applying the same concepts to both. Solutions of this general type have been defended by Wittgenstein and others. I do not know whether any of them have been successful. For our purposes that is not the important issue.

What is important is that we are not solipsists, and that the rejection of solipsism involves a capacity to view ourselves and our circumstances impersonally. All of our personal judgments, including first-person psychological claims, commit us to corresponding impersonal judgments about the same circumstances, viewed impersonally. Otherwise it would be impossible to apply the operative concepts to others in the same sense, and the supposition that there are other persons like oneself would be unintelligible. And if there are only certain types of personal judgments whose impersonal correlates we fail to acknowledge, then we shall be faced with a form of selective solipsism, or dissociation; for such claims would be dissociated from the idea of oneself as merely a person among others.

[1] The observations of this paragraph derive from Wittgenstein's *Philosophical Investigations* (Oxford: Blackwell, 1953), §§ 258–261.

5. The foregoing is not an adequate treatment of the problems of solipsism and other minds, any more than the earlier discussion of tenses and tenselessness was an adequate treatment of the metaphysics of time. But certain general conditions on the conception of a person have emerged, which can be applied to the category of practical judgments in much the same way as was possible with the earlier observations about time. This is because one can imagine an analogue of solipsism in the practical sphere: an inability to make practical judgments about other persons in the same sense in which one can make them in one's own case. We have considered the conditions which must be met by psychological concepts if they are to be applicable in the same sense to oneself and to others. We must now ask whether comparable conditions exist for practical judgments. What is it to accept the same judgment about another person that one accepts about oneself in acknowledging a reason to act, or in reaching a conclusion about what one should do?

To apply the judgment in the same sense to others, one must first be able to apply it to oneself conceived as merely one person among others. Only in that way is it guaranteed that what is judged does not apply only from a personal standpoint, and hence only to one's own case. So whenever one makes a personal practical judgment, like 'I should leave the building before the bomb goes off', this must carry with it a commitment to an impersonal practical judgment to the same effect about the person who one is. That impersonal judgment is equally implied by the judgments of others to the same effect about the same situation. And if the practical conclusion derives from certain features of the situation, the principles which govern that derivation must be statable impersonally, and so must the relevant conditions. One must for example be able to derive the conclusion that the individual should leave the building, from a specification of the probable effects of the bomb, the individual's vulnerability, and a principle that people should do what will keep them alive.

This yields a significant result, namely that one's basic practical principles must be universal. That is not a trivial claim; for it is not obvious why there should be any need to acknowledge, as the source of one's own reasons for action, a principle which applies to all persons. Why cannot each of us content himself with principles which state what *he* should do (principles like 'I should always act in my own interest') instead of expanding them into principles which yield reasons for everyone? The answer is that principles of the former type cannot be significantly applied to oneself from the impersonal standpoint; they therefore involve dissociation. To apply a principle to oneself impersonally, one must be able to apply it to the person who one is, in abstraction from the fact that it is oneself. And this cannot be done with a practical principle which applies *only* to oneself.

It is necessary to explain why this is so, for there are certain principles which appear at first glance to recast such private, one-person maxims in impersonal form. Consider the case of a non-universal but impersonal principle having to do with only one person: oneself impersonally identified. An example of such a principle would be 'T. N. should do what will keep him alive.' This may appear to be a plausible version of the impersonal principle behind the judgment 'I should do what will keep me alive', but it is not. For *being T.N.* is not one of the relevant conditions in the derivation of my *personal* practical judgments. That is, if I believe that I should get out of a burning building quickly, I generally believe that I should get out whether or not I am T.N.—i.e. even if I am only under the delusion that I am T.N. To add that identification as a premise of the corresponding impersonal practical judgment would be to alter the reasons for the judgment substantively, and not just by converting them from personal to impersonal form.[1]

The avoidance of dissociation therefore requires the acceptance of universal practical principles which apply in the same sense to everyone, and which are impersonally formulable, so that one can arrive at any true conclusion about what the persons in a situation should do, or have reason to do, without knowing what one's own place in the situation is, or indeed whether one occupies a place in it at all.

That is only the beginning, however, for we must ask next, what is the nature of the conclusions which these principles

[1] An analogous argument will work against impersonal principles like 'Everyone should do what will keep T.N. alive.' This principle, though both impersonal and universal, in the sense that it distributes reasons to everyone, is unacceptable as a basis for the impersonal analogue of the personal judgment, 'I should get out of this building.' It introduces as essential what the personal judgment regards as an irrelevant factor.

permit one to draw from the impersonal standpoint. What must these conclusions be like if they are to leave no residue of irreducibly personal practical judgments, which cannot be applied in the same sense to others? I wish to maintain that universality alone is not sufficient. In addition, the motivational content of ethical judgments must be present in their impersonal as well as their personal versions. It is not enough merely to be able to *say* of others, on impersonal grounds, what they should do. One must be able to mean by it what they mean when they make the same assertion. That is the basis for an interpretation of objective reasons.

6. In Chapter VIII I explained the sense in which first-person present-tense practical judgments possess motivational content; the acceptance of such a judgment is by itself sufficient to *explain* action or desire in accordance with it, although it is also compatible with the non-occurrence of such action or desire. I have referred to this motivational content as the *acceptance of a justification* for doing or wanting something. I argued that it must be present in first-person practical judgments, made from the standpoint of temporal neutrality, and hence also in judgments employing tenses other than the present. I shall now attempt to show by a similar argument that it must be present in impersonal practical judgments as well, and hence in judgments about what others should do.

If a practical judgment about one's own case consisted merely in the observation that certain features of one's situation fell into categories called 'reasons', then universality in the application of these categories would be sufficient to provide each personal practical judgment with an impersonal correlate differing from it only in the point of view from which it offered the same classification. But first-person practical judgments are not merely classificatory: they are judgments about what to do; they have practical consequences. If they were merely classificatory then a conclusion about what one *should* do would by itself have no bearing on a conclusion about what *to do*. The latter would have to be derived from the former, if at all, only with the aid of a further principle, about the reasonableness of doing what one should do. But then the original judgment about what one should do, or had reason to do, would have turned out not to be a practical judgment at all, but merely a classification belonging among the premises of the genuine practical judgment.

There seem to be three possible views of the relation between first-person practical judgments and motivation. (1) Judgments about what one should do have no role in the justification of motives, because motives cannot be justified. In that case the so-called practical judgments will not really be practical, though they may be causally associated with motives; i.e. it may happen that when an individual judges that he should do something, he often finds that he wants to do it, or does it. This would mean that the rational assessment of motives is impossible, which would not be granted even by an egoist. There seems at any rate no reason to believe it. (2) Judgments about what one should do, while themselves without motivational content, provide the premises for truly practical judgments, which depend on principles about what to do, given information about what one *should* do. This merely transfers all our problems to the category of principles about what to do, and the judgments which can be arrived at with their aid. How do those principles accord with the requirement of congruency between the two standpoints, and how can the motivational content of their first-person applications be included in impersonal versions of the same judgments? There seems no point in excluding motivational content from the original first-person practical conclusions, only to have it re-enter as the result of further practical reasoning. But if such an account should recommend itself for some reason, the same arguments about impersonal specifiability will apply, which apply on the assumption (3) that ordinary first-person practical judgments possess motivational content already. That is the position I take to be correct. First-person judgments about reasons are inherently relevant to decisions about what to do, and they provide the basis for justification and criticism of *action*, and *desire*—not just of judgments *about* action and desire.

I maintain that the first-person acknowledgment of a sufficient reason for doing something is the acknowledgment of a justification for doing it, and is sufficient to explain one's doing it. I do not wish to make a stronger claim than is necessary in this connection. There is no need to hold that 'X acknowledges a reason to A' *entails* 'X does A, or wants to do A,' or that the latter statement is part of the meaning of the former. Nor is it necessary to maintain that the first-person acknowledgment of a reason will produce a motivation unless other, contrary influences interfere. All I wish to claim is that such an acknowledgment is by itself *capable* of providing a motivation in the appropriate direction—that there is no need to seek an alternative or supplementary explanation of action when that one is available, and that in the absence of contrary influences or interferences this type of influence usually becomes operative.

What must be insisted upon is that while the motivational effects of such judgments are not invariable, they are considerable, and do not amount merely to pale modifications of affect. There may be certain evaluative principles whose motivational content is much weaker than that of practical judgments. There may be (though I doubt it) principles which give rise to nothing more than motivationally impotent feelings of approval or disapproval, whether in application to one's own case or to that of others. But this is irrelevant to the case we are considering, for we are considering reasons for *action* rather than principles of aesthetic assessment; and these specify not only the conditions in which it is rational to say or feel certain things about one's behaviour, but conditions in which it is rational to be motivated in certain ways—to want and to do things. The first-person acknowledgment of such a reason has significant motivational content.

Unless, therefore, some version of this motivational content can also be found in an impersonal practical judgment about the same situation, the principles which yield the first-person conclusion can be employed only at the cost of dissociation from the impersonal standpoint.

7. This is no more than a direct application to practical judgments of our earlier observation about other personal claims: that everything which they contain, with the single exception of a personal premise, can be comprehended in an impersonal view of the same circumstances. Thus 'the man sitting to my right has gout in his left foot' commits me to judgments about my position relative to a particular individual, about what will happen if I step hard on his left foot, what I can expect to hear,

etc. But the same situation can also be regarded impersonally, through a description of two persons sitting next to one another, and what one will feel and the other hear, etc., if the latter steps on the former's foot. The only personal judgment that cannot be so assimilated is the belief that I am the man on the left. This personal factor makes no difference in what is believed to be the case, or expected, but only in *how* it is believed or expected. (This is, to be sure, a formidable difference; the difference, e.g., between expecting that a particular man will feel excruciating pain and expecting to feel excruciating pain. But it is not a difference in what is expected to occur.)

How does this apply to a first-person, present-tense practical judgment? Suppose I am the man with gout, and I see the man to my left about to place his heel on my gouty toes. I conclude that I had better remove them to avoid the agony which will otherwise result, and I do. This much at least is clear: The judgment that T.N. has reason to remove his foot can be made in these circumstances impersonally; the action of removing them, on the other hand, relies on the personal standpoint, which permits a conclusion in the form of a decision to remove the foot, rather than that it should be removed. What is less clear, and what my argument is intended to settle, is whether any motivational content attaches to the impersonal judgment that T.N. has a reason to remove his foot, or whether it enters only with the addition of the basic personal premise, 'I am T.N.'

All of the conditions which provide the reason, and all of the principles which govern the operation of those conditions, can be specified impersonally. Suppose one arrives at a final impersonal practical judgment about the situation on this basis. And suppose that the resulting impersonal judgment has no motivational content whatever. Yet we know that once the personal premise is added, motivational content is present. Where then does it come from? If the judgment 'I should move my foot' is *justified*, motivational content and all, and the action itself is justified for the same reasons, then I must be adhering to a principle which warrants the adoption of motives, or the acceptance of justifications. But by the hypothesis under consideration it cannot be warranted on impersonal grounds (though the impersonal statement *that* a certain motive is warranted *can* be based entirely on impersonal grounds). So after passing completely through the procedures of justification and practical reasoning in impersonal terms I must apply a further, *personal* practical principle, which tells me, more or less, to care about what happens in cases where the reasons are mine. In other words, to reach a first-person judgment with motivational content requires a set of principles which connects each reason for a person to do something with a reason *to do* it, given the added premise that I am that person. The original, impersonal reasons do not possess the motivational content necessary to permit the conversion from a reason *that* someone should do something into a reason *to* do it, upon the addition of the basic personal premise that I am that someone.

This is the equivalent of solipsism in the sphere of practical reasoning. For it means that an essential aspect of the first-person judgment, namely the acceptance of a justification, is not present in the impersonal correlate of the same judgment. A non-solipsist who switches from the expectation that a certain impersonally specified individual will feel pain in his foot, to the expectation of pain in his own foot, upon adding the premise that he is that individual, does not thereby alter his expectation of what will occur, but only the point of view from which he expects the same occurrence.[1] But someone whose impersonal practical judgments lack motivational content cannot accept a justification for wanting or promoting anything impersonally conceived, on purely impersonal grounds, and consequently cannot pass from accepting a justification for something thus conceived to accepting a justification for the same thing conceived personally. What is already present in the impersonal practical judgment that individual X should do Y does not allow the practical solipsist to convert to the acceptance of a justification *for doing Y*, given the information that he is X. It is as if, in the non-practical case, someone were unable to pass from the expectation that X will shortly feel a sharp pain in his foot, to the expectation of a sharp pain in the foot, given only the additional information that he is X. It is as if a special conversion

---

[1] Even if the added premise gives him further information about the occurrence, such as that the pain will be felt by a 140-lb. male citizen of the U.S., this too could have been incorporated in the impersonal expectation from the start.

principle were required in addition, correlating expectation of sharp pains in someone's foot with expectation of a special kind of event, should that someone be myself. But such a principle, if not itself susceptible to impersonal reformulation, is the essence of solipsism, and its practical analogue is practical solipsism.

I call it practical solipsism, because it is an inability to draw fully-fledged practical conclusions about impersonally viewed situations. If the impersonal analogues of one's first-person practical judgments lack motivational content, then one cannot make the *same* judgment about a situation from the impersonal standpoint which one makes about that situation from the personal standpoint. If one could, then it would be possible to pass from the impersonal to the personal form without an alteration in the content of the judgment, but only an alteration in its point of view. For example, one could pass from the acceptance of a justification for wanting an impersonally described act to occur, to acceptance of a justification for wanting *to do* it, with the introduction of the basic personal premise and nothing more. This is an extremely important shift, but it is not a shift in the judgment being made about the act—only a shift in the point of view from which that act is regarded. If, on the other hand, the impersonal judgment possesses no motivational content, then the mere addition of the basic personal premise cannot yield a true first-person practical conclusion, for the shift which that would demand is much more radical; it has to do with the content of one's judgment about the situation rather than with the point of view from which that situation is being regarded. A motivationally weightless impersonal judgment can only turn into a motivationally weightless personal judgment upon the addition of the basic personal premise. To justify the presence of motivational content in the conclusion, one would need a further practical principle, capable only of personal formulation.

 What is the alternative? Solipsism is avoided in non-practical areas if everything which can be stated, asserted, expected, believed, judged from a personal standpoint can be similarly viewed from the impersonal standpoint. A comparable result would be achieved in the practical sphere by a system of reasons permitting impersonal practical judgments corresponding to all our personal ones—the former being conclusions to the same effect about the same matters conceived impersonally rather than personally. This does not mean that our practical reasoning must be conducted in impersonal terms, and that we can arrive at a personal conclusion only by first reaching an impersonal judgment and then shifting to the personal standpoint. (That *may* happen, but it is obviously an uncommon occurrence.) It is necessary only that we be *able* to cast our practical reasonings in impersonal form. There is no difference in this respect between the practical case and others; we do not generally arrive at personal conclusions about matters of fact by reasoning in impersonal terms and then converting to the first person at the final step. But we are committed to the truth of the relevant impersonal principles, whether we consciously employ them or not. And in the practical case, that is a strong enough requirement to rule out purely subjective reasons, as I shall explain in the next chapter.

XII

THE INTERPRETATION OF OBJECTIVE REASONS

1. It must now be shown that objective reasons avoid practical solipsism while subjective reasons do not. Let us begin with the latter claim. The conclusions of the previous chapter enable us to show that a subjective practical principle does not permit one to make the same judgments about others that one makes about oneself, or the same judgments about oneself viewed impersonally that one makes about oneself viewed personally. The application of subjective reasons involves a dissociation of the two standpoints, and a breach in the conception of oneself as just a person among others.

This may not be immediately obvious because in certain respects subjective reasons seem in accord with congruency of the two standpoints. The typical subjective principle is both universal and impersonally formulated. It applies to everyone, and *a fortiori* to me, since I am someone. And since it does not distinguish between persons within its range according to whether they are me or not, it can be applied impersonally to the individual who I in fact am, without that fact having any bearing on the result. Just as the principle will yield conclusions about what others have reason to do, so it can yield conclusions about what *that* person has reason to do—employing no additional premises beyond those drawn from the impersonally specifiable features of his situation.

The difficulty is, however, that an individual's impersonally derived attitude toward his own acts in consequence of a universal subjective principle can be no different from his attitude toward any other person's acts, except in so far as this is warranted, on the principle, by *impersonally* specified differences between himself and others. And subjective principles do not warrant judgments or attitudes with motivational content concerning acts or states of affairs viewed impersonally. That is the core of the problem. Because of its free agent-variable, a subjective principle can justify only a desire for things bearing a certain relation to *oneself*: one's interests, the interests of one's family or country, etc. And although it provides that justification for everyone, to accept the justification in one's own case requires that the end to which the principle applies be identified *personally*. If I merely consider in impersonal terms the individual who I in fact am, I can conclude that there is, for him, subjective reason to do this or that, but this does not involve, and cannot even explain, any desire that he do so. The motivational content which forms an essential part of a first-person practical judgment is therefore missing entirely from an impersonal judgment about the same individual, if that judgment derives from a subjective principle. Moreover, since the very same subjective principle will yield conclusions with motivational content when applied to my own case in the first person, the dissociation of the two standpoints is apparent in the operation of the principle itself.

It should be remarked that congruency between the standpoints cannot be achieved by anything less than acceptance of a justification for wanting or promoting the relevant end, when the reason has been impersonally acknowledged. It will not do to suggest that some other form of affect, such as a motivationally impotent approval or disapproval, can be justified by the impersonal acceptance of subjective reasons. For mere approval of a course of action impersonally described has as its personal analogue mere approval of the same action conceived in the first person—and that is different from acceptance of a justification for performing the action. The impersonal analogue of accepting a justification for wanting to do something is accepting a justification for wanting it to be done by the person who one is. Subjective principles, impersonally applied, do not support such conditions.

It is futile to argue that an impersonal judgment can contain the appropriate attitudes in hypothetical form. The suggestion would be that my application of a subjective principle to a particular person (impersonally specified) includes the provision that *if* I am that person, then I should act in the way prescribed (with all the motivational content that judgment implies). But such an account fails to preserve the impersonal view, for the motivational content of the general subjective principle has now become simply: 'For each person, if I am that person, then I should act as the principle prescribes for him.' But that is nothing more than the personal maxim that *I* should do as the principle says. Since no impersonal attitudes to one's actions can derive from such a maxim, nothing has been done towards meeting the congruency condition.

These are straightforward consequences of any subjective principle, egoism included. The conclusions regarding justification of attitudes towards the actions of others belong to the *point* of egoism: that it is rational to care about what one has reason to do oneself, but not rational to care at all about the reasons of others. I have simply brought this feature of subjective reasons to bear on the case of one's own action, impersonally regarded. Such reasons do not permit practical engagement from the impersonal standpoint.[1]

2. Though I have referred to the result as practical solipsism, it should be clear that a restriction to subjective reasons would not have to be allied with a more general solipsism. This means that the impersonal standpoint would be available, and that one could always adopt it, at the cost of abandoning those practical judgments which subjective reasons permit from the personal standpoint.

It is useful to consider the attendant dissociation from this point of view. If one is always in a position to adopt the impersonal standpoint, viewing oneself as merely another inhabitant of the world, then it will always be possible to step backwards out of one's life, as it were; out of the life of activity and practical concerns. All of one's concerns, desires, and justifica-

---

[1] This is not controverted by the fact, pointed out in Ch. X, §3, that egoism and other subjective reasons can bring different persons to acknowledge common goals. It might be thought that if certain goals are subjectively desirable to everyone, this reintroduces congruency between the two standpoints, for a man can be justified on subjective principles in wanting these goals, even if he does not know who he is. This might seem equivalent to wanting them impersonally. But first of all, there will be numerous matters remaining on which agreement is unreachable, so one will still have to know who one is to know what practical judgments to accept. Secondly, the condition of not knowing who one is is not the same as the impersonal standpoint, for the latter does not imply that one is *any* of the persons in the scene being viewed. It abstracts from such considerations entirely. An egoistic preference exercised under the condition of ignorance, on the other hand, does assume that one is (or at least may be) *in* the world under consideration, and susceptible therefore to the effects of one's choice.

tions will themselves be included within the scope of the impersonal view, but when one views this entire phenomenon impersonally, one will be unable to care whether what one cares about personally happens or not. The ascent to the impersonal standpoint gives one an overview from which everything appears indifferent. And this is a step which can always be taken. Consequently, if certain practical conclusions can be reached only from the personal standpoint, there is *no* position safely out of the range of a higher vantage point from which everything appears indifferent—no viewpoint yielding concerns which cannot be lost in a still more comprehensive overview—and therefore no source of concern which involves the entire person unequivocally. With personal-impersonal dissociation the possibility of disengagement is always present.

The fact is that neither of the two standpoints can be eliminated from our view of the world, and when one of them cannot accept the judgments of the other, we are faced with a situation in which the individual is not operating as a unit. Two sides of the idea of himself, and hence two sides of himself, are coming apart. The only principles which avoid this result in the practical sphere are objective ones.

3. Objective and subjective principles resemble one another in being universal and impersonally formulated; so both allow one to *say* what anyone (oneself included) has reason to do, on the basis of either personal, or impersonal premises. When this conclusion is derived from an objective principle, however, it is the same practical judgment, with the same motivational content, whether it is arrived at from the personal or the impersonal standpoint.

Only objective principles warrant either willingness to promote an end, or a desire for that end, when a reason is seen to apply to that end impersonally conceived. That is because objective reasons do not contain a free agent-variable, so nothing about one's relation to the end need be considered in deciding whether the reason applies. If one acknowledges the presence of an objective reason for something, one has acknowledged a reason for *anyone* to promote or desire its occurrence—at *least* to desire it, even if he is not in a position to do anything about the matter. This is because objective reasons represent the values

of occurrences, acts, and states of affairs themselves, not their
values *for* anyone. Since they ascribe non-relative desirability to
events or circumstances, impersonally described, it follows that
they retain their motivational content when applied impersonally; so the condition of congruency is met.

Objective practical judgments can be relativistic in the following sense: what is judged objectively desirable may itself be
some relation, perhaps between persons or between a person and
something else. And the relation may be such that anyone other
than the person or persons involved is in a poor position to promote or facilitate its success. This possibility is very important,
and some of its consequences for the character of a system of
objective principles will be discussed in the next chapter.
Nevertheless, even if a relation of this character has been judged
objectively desirable, it can still be impersonally regarded; and
the same practical judgment, with its motivational content, remains valid whether one is involved in the relation or not. The
effect of adding the personal premise will be in what the judgment persuades one to *do* about the matter. It may be, if a
personal relation is involved, that unless one is involved in the
relation oneself there is not much one *can* do to promote the
occurrences to which the objective reason applies. In that case
one will be restricted to non-interference in the efforts of those
who are involved.

Considerable variety is possible in the type of impersonally
specified end to which objective reasons can apply, and it may
not always be immediately obvious to what one should assign
objective value, in each case in which an individual has a reason
to do something. But if that reason derives from an objective
principle, then there must be some feature of the situation which
can engage the practical judgment of anyone, complete with
motivational content, whether he is in a position to interfere or
not. There must be something for whose occurrence there is a
reason.[1]

[1] As I have said earlier, there is no need in this argument to distinguish between
a reason for something simply to occur, and a reason for anyone at all to want it to
occur. Perhaps all reasons are fundamentally reasons for people to do and want
things, and objective reasons are distinguished from subjective ones simply by the
range of their influence. Nevertheless an objective principle provides reasons for
everyone to desire a common goal in a different way from a subjective reason which
happens to yield a common goal for everyone. The latter depends on some appro-

4. I have said something in the previous chapter about the fact that action necessarily involves the personal standpoint. One cannot in general decide what to do unless one knows something about who one is. We must consider that matter again now, for it threatens to create difficulties for the contention that objective reasons guarantee congruency between the two standpoints.

To begin with, it may be held that without the possibility of action there can be no desire, and hence no motivational content in any judgment. If that were so, then the impersonal standpoint could not yield any practical judgments with motivational content, and that method of distinguishing between subjective and objective judgments would be impossible. My reply to this is that although desire usually involves a willingness to act, should appropriate means be available, it need not involve action proper, and may be unaccompanied by any thought of action. After all, it is possible to want something to have happened in the past, without believing one can do anything to bring it about.

Moreover a desire need not be formulated in the first person. Normally one expresses a desire by saying 'I want (or wish, or hope) X.' But it can also be expressed impersonally, in the form 'Would that X' or 'If only X.' Why can there not be desires which are completely impersonal in the sense that their objects and their grounds are formulated in completely impersonal terms? Such a desire might imply a readiness to adopt measures to promote its object, but it would imply nothing whatever about the availability of any such means, or one's relation to that object. If that can be true of a desire, there is no reason to think otherwise of the typical motivational content of a practical judgment, which is not actually a desire, but only the acceptance of a *justification* for desiring or promoting a given end.

It remains the case that actions do result when one supplements a practical judgment with the personal standpoint, and we must explain how the reasoning which leads to those actions can be accommodated from the impersonal standpoint. Suppose that an objective reason is acknowledged to attach to a certain

---

priate relation between each of the individuals and the end in question, whereas the former does not. Thus what has objective value is not thereby of value *to* anyone— not even to everyone.

end, so that I accept a justification for desiring or promoting that end, impersonally described. To be motivated to action or to accept a justification for action on this ground, I must believe that certain acts available to me will promote that end. That is of course an item of personal information. However, the relevant relations between those acts and the end can be impersonally specified, and the acts themselves impersonally conceived. Therefore everything necessary to yield a justification for acting can be impersonally acknowledged with the exception of the basic personal premise. Reasoning impersonally, one can arrive not only at the judgment that there is a reason to want the end, but also at the judgment that this gives a particular person reason to do certain things which will promote that end. One can make this judgment, moreover, about one's own actions, impersonally conceived; and if the judgment is objective, it will possess motivational content even though one does not conceive the actions as one's own. The judgment that T.N. has objective reason to do X involves acceptance of a justification for wanting T.N. to do X, which becomes, with the addition of the information that I am T.N., acceptance of a justification for doing X. All the steps in practical reasoning from objective principles, down to the identification of appropriate courses of action, can be impersonally represented, with the sole omission being the basic personal premise. That is enough to avoid the practical analogue of solipsism, for although the shift to the personal standpoint is a radical one (the shift from wanting *that* to wanting *to* is as radical as the shift from expecting *that* to expecting *to*), and although it puts one in a position to act, it does not represent a change in one's judgments about the situation or about those acts which, as it turns out, one is in a position to perform.

The same cannot be said of a subjective principle. If a subjective principle is applied impersonally, one may be able to *select* those acts of the individual one happens to be, which are justified by the subjective principle. But this is a mere classification without motivational content—without the acceptance of a justification for wanting anything. Therefore when one adds the personal premise, the resulting introduction of such content is much more than a change in point of view. It is an additional judgment about the same situation, which can be made only from the personal standpoint. Although I might appear in such a case to be acting on an impersonal universal principle which specifies subjective reasons, I could not be acting on the impersonal principle alone, because that principle warrants no motivationally weighted conclusions about my acts impersonally conceived. Hence it cannot warrant acceptance of justifications *for acting*, when the point of view shifts and I regard those acts as mine. A further principle is necessary to warrant such conclusions, and it will have to be a purely personal one.

Objective principles avoid dissociation because, in their application, the derivation of a justification *for acting* depends only on a shift of standpoint; everything else is derivable impersonally. And that one residue, the basic personal premise which permits action, is logically unavoidable and therefore does not constitute a *failure* of integration between the two standpoints. It is simply an essential aspect of the distinction between them.

5. The conclusion reached so far is in many ways a limited one. Objective and subjective are entirely *formal* categories, and the substantive consequences of a restriction to objective reasons have yet to be discussed. That will be done in the next chapter.

Moreover it must be repeated that an interpretation of the kind I have offered is neither a justification of the conduct which it explains, nor a demonstration that such conduct is necessary. It is not a justification, because a justification must operate within the framework of an assumed system of reasons for action, and this interpretation offers to explain the most fundamental structure of just such a system. It is not a demonstration of necessity, because it is possible to imagine an individual fully capable of occupying the impersonal standpoint and possessing a conception of himself as just another of the world's inhabitants, who nevertheless remained from this standpoint split off, detached from his practical concerns and his rationally motivated actions. Personal egoism is not unimaginable. It merely entails an inability to extend to others, or to oneself impersonally regarded, the types of practical judgment which one can make in the first person.

Objective principles, on the other hand, do permit fully-fledged practical conclusions about oneself viewed impersonally, and therefore also about others (for it is the impersonal content which is common). Thus the argument explains the sense in which a concern for the interests of others depends on a full recognition of their reality. That recognition is possible only if one can view oneself impersonally; but it will be incomplete unless one's practical principles are objective, for only objective principles permit practical judgments from the impersonal standpoint. And it is through the acknowledgment of objective reasons that one can arrive at a justified concern for the interests of others, independent of one's relation to them.

This result stands even though we are often weak, cowardly, self-deceiving, and insensitive to the reality of other persons. There is never a lack of explanations for human lapses from ideally rational conduct, and when the stakes are high, the temptations of solipsistic dissociation are considerable. It is often a struggle to maintain the clear sense of oneself as just a person among others. But I have not maintained that human conduct invariably accords with that conception. I have only tried to explain our deep-seated susceptibility to non-egoistic reasons, and our capacity to recognize them as requirements if the issue is forced upon us with sufficient clarity.[1]

---

[1] Nothing is more natural than the desire to substitute someone else for oneself as the victim of misfortune; and nothing is more natural than to think "Thank god it isn't me", when disaster strikes someone else. But I contend that to *act* on such grounds is contrary to reason, as it requires the acceptance of justifications which cannot be impersonally acknowledged.

XIII

THE CONSEQUENCES

1. Although it is not my aim to produce a detailed system of moral conclusions, it is necessary to say *something* about the substantive consequences derivable from the formal requirement of objective reasons which has been defended here. This is appropriate both because the results are intrinsically interesting and because the plausibility of an ethical theory may be thought to depend partly on the intuitive acceptability of its moral consequences. It is essential at least to argue that the consequences of a principle of objectivity are not obviously unacceptable.

I have already observed that the conclusion reached so far, while extremely general, is nevertheless limited; it only places a *formal* condition on reasons of whatever kind—the condition of objectivity. No restrictions have yet been placed on the content of those reasons and principles which may satisfy this formal condition. Furthermore, all such principles specify conditions for the presence of *prima facie* reasons; they do not inform us how to derive from these preliminary conclusions decisive results about what should be done. It remains to be seen: (a) whether these limited formal results can be made to yield important substantive restrictions on what can serve as a reason; and (b) what further premises are necessary to derive the consequence that certain things *must* serve as reasons. It may be possible to derive partial answers to these questions from the requirement of congruency which underlies the objectivity condition itself.

First let us consider what is implied by the fact that the condition of objectivity is entirely formal. It is evident that an enormous number of reasons of varying plausibility can satisfy the condition. A fanatic who recognized no reasons for action other than those dictated by respect for a certain deity would be meeting the congruency condition, so long as those reasons were objectively formulable and universally binding—for he would accept no reasons for action from the personal standpoint which could not be accepted from the impersonal standpoint.

It is clear, in fact, that any catalogue of values can be put into objective form. Whatever one may regard as a legitimate goal of action might in principle be regarded as an objective goal—one which anyone had reason to promote. Therefore the formal condition of objectivity cannot dispense with a substantive theory of value, and that is something I have not attempted to construct.

However, as I tried to indicate in Chapter VIII, §7, certain substantive results seem to derive support from considerations related to those which underlie the requirements of objectivity and timelessness: namely, considerations having to do with dissociation and its avoidance. For example, it is natural to say of the religious fanatic imagined above, who excludes all reasons except for a few eccentric ones, that he is rationally dissociated from his natural desires and the demands of his body. Although no dissociation of standpoints reveals itself *within* his rational deliberations, the entire apparatus of practical reason is dissociated from his natural desires and bodily impulses. He must regard them all as alien influences to which he can attend only to inhibit them. Certainly he will not identify with his natural desires, as most of us do.

Dissociation of this type is rare. Most people do not regard themselves as passengers in their bodies, and are motivated rather than assaulted by their natural impulses. Therefore we need not hesitate to regard as given a certain range of subjective reasons derived from the natural desires. It would be difficult to specify those reasons exactly; they vary somewhat from person to person, and they are not associated exclusively with satisfaction, but also with the more complex notion of interest. Nevertheless, it is in application to such considerations that the congruency requirement yields significant results, in the form of objective reasons for concerning oneself with other people. I do not wish to deny that there are other reasons as well—reasons which do not derive in any way from natural human desires. But one would need a theory of value to be able to specify their content, and I have not sought to supply one. I wish only to illustrate the consequences of objectification by reference to the case of certain subjective reasons which have a natural plausibility.

After indicating the sources of straightforward altruism, I

shall discuss some of the factors which modify its effects and make the consequences of a requirement of objectivity more complicated than one might initially suppose. (It will emerge, for example, that objective principles can permit the situation of an agent to limit the reasons which he should take into account.)

2. The possibility of simple altruism depends on acknowledgment of a special type of subjective reason, and its submission to the procedure of objectification. The relevant subjective reasons are those which attach to the satisfaction of certain of one's needs and interests *per se*, without too much concern over the source of that satisfaction.

This is by no means true of all interests, and the character of an objective principle depends to a great extent on the character of the subjective reason from which it derives. If the proper ends of human life are understood in a sufficiently eccentric fashion, their objective correlates may be equally eccentric. For example, the condition of objectivity could be met by principles of conduct which demanded the fiercest self-reliance and competitiveness of all individuals, positively forbidding them either to assist each other or to accept assistance in overcoming difficulty, and enjoining them only to continue the struggle for survival or domination, and to see that others continued it as well. Such a position would follow from the objectification of a view of individual interest which made struggle, competition, and danger the primary subjective goals.[1]

But not all reasons are so involuted. At least sometimes objectification will demand that everyone pursue an uncomplicated end which we already acknowledge a subjective reason to pursue; the elimination of pain, for example, or survival, or the satisfaction of basic appetites. If this is the case, then we have prima facie reason to secure those ends for others as well as for ourselves. That is not to deny that there may be reasons to secure them for ourselves and those closely related to us; various factors may complicate the result when there is conflict between reasons to help others and reasons to help oneself. But even if we allow for these possibilities, the acknowledgment of prima facie

[1] A caricature of Nietzsche's position might take such a form, and that is instructive in one respect: it suggests that he is not an egoist. Such values as he admits are objective rather than subjective.

reasons to help others is a significant result. It means at least
this: that when one can secure or promote such an end for
someone else, and either (a) there are no conflicting reasons, or
(b) all other considerations balance out, then one has sufficient
reason to act. The reason is *simply* that one's act will promote the
other's survival, eliminate his suffering, or what have you. It
depends on no desire or interest of the agent—only on the
objectivity of certain reasons which he acknowledges subjectively. This is a non-trivial result (however rarely the circumstances described may be thought to arise), and an acceptable
one. It is neither paradoxical nor counter-intuitive to maintain
that one automatically has a reason to help someone in need if
there is no reason not to.

3. A number of other factors complicate the procedure of
objectification. They fall into three categories. First, there is
great variation in the character of plausible subjective reasons,
and their objectification will therefore not always take a simple
altruistic form. Second, there can be objective justification for
restrictions on the objective reasons which an individual should
consider in certain contexts. Third, there must be combinatorial
principles to settle conflicts between prima facie objective
reasons arising from the interests of different persons; nothing
has yet been said about their nature. In this section and the next
we shall consider matters of the first two types. The rest of the
chapter will be taken up with the combinatorial problem.

First of all, not all human interests are possible objects of
direct altruism. Objectification would be a relatively simple
matter if an individual's interests could all be straightforwardly
defined in terms of the satisfaction of his desires, or of some
sub-set thereof. In that case the respect which objective reasons
demand for the interests of others would reduce itself to consideration of their desires, and the only problem remaining would
concern the settlement of interpersonal conflicts. But it is by no
means obvious that such a close connection exists between
interest and desire, or even that desire is among the most important determinants of interest. It may be just as important to
have certain desires or to avoid others; and the satisfaction of
desires which it is contrary to one's interest to possess, may itself
be contrary to one's interest.

A deeper complication is the following. Human life consists

not primarily in the passive reception of stimuli, pleasant or unpleasant, satisfying or dissatisfying; it consists to a significant degree in activities and pursuits. If one passes beyond the most basic needs, the reasons a person has to conduct his life in certain ways are not reasons simply to bring about certain ends, which might be brought about *for* him just as well. They are reasons for active pursuits and involvements, which cannot be adequately carried forward on his behalf by another person. For the most part he must live his own life; others are not in a position to live it for him, nor is he in a position to lead theirs. Sometimes, indeed, attempts at positive assistance will themselves constitute objectionable interference, if the activity is one in which autonomy, spontaneity, and originality are important. People who are painting, or writing poetry, or making love, will usually be ungrateful for assistance.

It is evident that when such activities are governed by reasons, the objective versions of those reasons, even if they assign objective value to the activities in question, will not yield an immediate requirement of concern for the *goals* someone else has reason to pursue. Not only is one usually in a better practical position to look after one's own interests, but there are certain ends and objects which one is in a *logically* better position to pursue for oneself than for others.

The proper form of objectification depends on the nature of the subjective reasons with which one begins. At one end of the spectrum is a subjective goal like the elimination of physical pain, which can be objectified directly, since a mere end to pain, rather than any activity of pain-elimination, appears to be our sole aim in subjectively motivated pain avoidance. Satisfaction of the basic appetites provides us with a more complicated case, for although the passive acceptance of such benefits from the hands of others is regarded as subjectively desirable, it may be more desirable to engage actively in the procurement of that satisfaction. The objective correlates of such reasons will be correspondingly complex. They will justify a certain amount of direct beneficence, but will also reveal a bias towards looking after one's own needs and making it possible for others to look after theirs. Finally, in matters such as the conduct of intimate personal relations, artistic creation, and the pursuit of a career, the most important consequence of objectification will be that we have reason to avoid interference with others in their devotion to such concerns. Reasons to make common cause with them will be much rarer.

These observations bear on the conditions of behavior in social units, particularly small social units like the family. To the extent that one's role in a social unit is based on relations, especially intimate relations, it becomes likely that the un-hindered and spontaneous performance of that role is an end in itself. Consequently the welfare and happiness of one's family, for example, are not ends entirely detachable from one's own pursuit of them (though, to be sure, one has reason to desire that they should be secured by whatever means may be available). Concern for one's wife and children is not merely concern for the welfare of some people whom one happens to be in a convenient position to help. Consequently, the objecti-fication of the reasons in whose acknowledgment this concern finds rational embodiment will not yield equal reasons to con-cern oneself with the wives and children of others (although a perfectly general altruism will certainly yield some consequences in that direction).

It should be emphasized that this type of restriction on the consequences of objectification does not reduce it to vacuity in such cases. The principle still yields objective rather than merely subjective reasons for people to look after their families. And even if one would defeat those reasons by directly assisting or forcing others to conform to them, two important conse-quences remain: there are reasons to avoid interference with others engaged in such activities, and also reasons to seek the social, economic, and political conditions which make such pursuits possible, not only for oneself but for others.

Similar conditions govern the conduct of larger and looser associations: clubs, businesses, even nations.[1] While their rea-sons to pursue their own goals and look after their own members may be such that a good deal of legitimate self-involvement is preserved under objectification, individuals involved in such

[1] Religions present a more complex case. Since the adherents of one religion may not recognize that the adherents of another religion, which they regard as false, have even subjective reason to adhere to its practices, the consequences of objectification are unclear. However, a more complicated argument may well yield principles of tolerance for such cases. (Cf. John Rawls, 'Constitutional Liberty and the Concept of Justice', *Nomos*, VI (1963).)

associations are nevertheless bound to acknowledge objective reasons for other groups of a similar kind to pursue similar goals, with the consequence that they must acknowledge reasons (a) to avoid interference with those pursuits if possible, and (b) to seek the kind of social or international order which will facilitate such pursuits. Pure egoism among nations is no more defensible than it is among individuals.

4. We have not yet mentioned what is perhaps the primary factor operating to maintain the importance of one's personal position in a system of objective reasons: the phenomenon of competition. Competitions of various kinds permeate our lives and institutions. At first glance they appear to provide classic examples of subjective reasons which cannot admit objective correlates. I believe that this is an illusion, and that it will emerge upon examination that objective principles underlie the reasons governing individual conduct in competitive situations. This reveals something important about the operation of objective principles.

Consider a boxing match. Each of the two fighters has reason to try to knock the other out and prevent the other from knocking him out, to employ his own strength and skill to best advantage and to prevent his opponent from doing so. At the same time he will agree that his opponent has similar reasons. It is evidently absurd to suggest that, in agreeing to this, he is acknowledging a justification for wanting or helping his opponent to succeed. This creates the impression that the operative reasons are irreducibly subjective.

I wish to suggest that there are patently *objective* reasons for each fighter to pursue his own success without the slightest consideration for his opponent. These derive from the objective reasons for holding the match in the first place. It is designed to give both contestants the opportunity of competitive victory and perhaps financial gain, and also to give spectators the pleasure of watching such a contest. These ends are ill served if the fighters assist each other. One cannot win a victory over a complaisant opponent. Certain limits to the outcome are set by the foul rules, heavy boxing gloves, and the presence of a physician who can stop the fight on medical grounds. But within those limits it is essential to the objective point of the

match that the contestants themselves concentrate only on winning. Nothing else is compatible with their role. The considerations which activate them therefore appear purely subjective, but it is possible to offer an objective justification for this, though I do not contend that such a justification is running through the average prize-fighter's head as he pummels his opponent into insensibility.

This type of objectively justified restriction on the types of reasons which one is prepared to consider is extremely common, and it transcends the phenomena of competition. Competition itself is omnipresent, not only in sports and games, but in business, politics, the law, and sometimes even the arts. Lawyers do not assist the arguments of their opponents in court; that is not the point of the adversary method. Even where competition and the chance to win are not the main point of a procedure, they may be essential to its success in achieving what *is* its main point. Thus when a defender of the competitive economy wishes to appeal to the general good, he argues that the general good is best served if no one pursues it and everyone concentrates only on his own profit.

The existence of objective reasons against considering objective reasons is merely one example of an exceedingly common phenomenon. Reasons of a given sort continually require their own suppression. The only way to run downstairs is not to try, you cannot make her love you by doing what you think will make her love you, you will not impress the interviewer unless you stop trying to impress him. Principles of this sort are often true, and in our earlier discussion of prudence we came across another: that exclusive concern for one's long-term advantage is not to one's long-term advantage. It should therefore not be surprising that there is objective justification for restrictions on the consideration of objective reasons, both in the context of competitive practices and elsewhere. The examples I have offered are intended only to suggest how the appearance of irreducible subjectivity can be removed in other cases. I think it is not unreasonable to believe that such considerations will make it possible to accommodate the subtleties of practical reason under objective principles, though I cannot even begin such a project here.

The demands of objectification are therefore complex, but

not trivial. They will almost certainly include a requirement of straightforward interpersonal altruism, in matters of basic human need. We all have reason to help people who are starving and to prevent them from being filled with shrapnel or coated with napalm—even if they do not happen to be relatives, friends, or fellow countrymen.

5. The limitations on pure altruism sketched so far concern primarily the respects in which, despite the objectivity of reasons, an individual is justified in paying more attention to his own problems and to the needs of those close to him than to the problems of humanity at large. I now wish to turn to a problem which does not depend on the relevance of one's specific place in the scene under consideration, and which arises whatever else we may have settled about the objective reasons bearing on the situation.

It must be remembered that the procedure of objectification described so far yields only *prima facie* reasons for considering the interests of others, when it yields any at all. To pass from prima facie reasons to conclusions about what to do, one needs combinatorial principles which will yield a decision when the prima facie reasons conflict, as they do in almost every case. Nothing has been said about these combinatorial principles.

Of course nothing has been said either about how conflicts between prima facie reasons are to be resolved on the purely subjective level, and some of the problems about interpersonal combination might be dealt with by importing combinatorial methods directly from the subjective to the objective system. Or it might be thought that the process of objectification, when applied to subjective combinatorial principles, would somehow yield combinatorial principles adequate to deal with conflicts between prima facie objective reasons.

I believe the solution is not as simple as that. The reasons for this can be seen without a knowledge of the actual combinatorial principles governing subjective reasons.[1] For suppose that there are some principles for the individual case, assigning relative weights to different types of reasons, taking probabilities

[1] Little work has been done on the formulation of those principles. Recently, however, Robert Nozick has arrived at important conclusions about the balance of conflicting *moral* reasons. See 'Moral Complications and Moral Structures' *Natural Law Forum* 13 (1968)—a paper which may have started an exact science within the subject of ethics.

and desirabilities into account, and enabling us to assess the rationality of risks. Even without specifying those principles, it seems clear that if the subjective reasons whose combination they govern must be objectified, so must the combinatorial principles. But this implies only that when we are presented with several conflicting objective reasons stemming from the interests of another person, we must weigh them *against one another* by the same principles which it would be rational for that individual to employ in weighing the subjective reasons from which they originate.

This says nothing, however, about what principles are to be employed in settling conflicts between objective reasons stemming from the interests of *different* persons. When I consider a varied assortment of reasons stemming from another's interest I must apply the same decision function that he could rationally apply to them himself. It does not follow, however, that I can apply this same function to a collection of reasons stemming from both our interests, or from his interests and those of someone else. It appears in fact unlikely that the objective versions even of sophisticated intrapersonal combinatorial principles can be applied to interpersonal problems.

This difficulty is not limited to the settlement of conflicts between one's own interests and those of others; it applies to conflict between the interests of any two (or more) persons. The defect of any direct application to the interpersonal case of the objective correlate of a subjective combinatorial principle is that it fails to take seriously the distinction between persons. It treats the desires, needs, satisfactions, and dissatisfactions of distinct persons as if they were the desires, etc., of a mass person. But this is to ignore the *significance* of the fact (when it is a fact) that the members of a set of conflicting desires and interests all fall within the boundaries of a single life, and can be dealt with as the claims of a single individual. Conflicts between the interests of distinct individuals, on the other hand, must be regarded in part as conflicts between *lives*; and that is a very different matter.[1]

---

[1] This very important point is central to John Rawls's recent work on justice. It appears in the final section of the essay 'Constitutional Liberty and the Concept of Justice', cited above, and receives more extensive treatment in material distributed to his classes at Harvard in 1965 and 1967. The same point is made by David Gauthier, on page 126 of *Practical Reasoning* (Oxford, 1963).

6. Where then can we discover combinatorial principles governing interpersonal conflict? Without offering an explicit solution,
I should like to suggest that such principles can be arrived at
only by further application of the congruency condition and the
requirement of objectivity which follows from it. We must now
speculate about what those conditions might be applied to, in
order to yield a satisfactory result.

The problem is posed by conflicts arising from the initial
objectification of subjective reasons which are already acknowledged. If we now add to these data the condition that there
must be *some* method for resolving those conflicts, we are presented with a new object for subjectively motivated preferences and
for the application of subjective principles. It is through the
objectification of *these subjective* reasons for preference among
methods of combining prima facie objective reasons that we
must seek to construct objective principles of combination.

Individuals will differ, however, in the combinatorial principles which they find subjective reasons for preferring. It is not
self-evidently possible to discover a subjective preference
operating in such circumstances which *can* be objectified, and
which will resolve the conflict instead of merely reproducing it
at a new level.

Certain preferences can be ruled out of the running immediately, on the ground that their objectifications are self-
contradictory. It seems probable, for example, that for any
individual considering the matter subjectively, the most appealing combinatorial principles are those which single him out for
preferential treatment in case of conflict between himself and
anyone else. However, the objective version of any such principle would state that everyone should receive preferential treatment in case of conflict; and that would be a contradiction.

For this reason we cannot consider any subjectively attractive
principles which single out one individual for special treatment.
The choice will therefore be restricted to principles that are
already objective and impersonal. But although any subjective
preference for a combinatorial principle of that kind will at
least be objectifiable without contradiction, it will not solve our
problem. The conflict will reappear if different persons, in
choosing among the possible objective interpersonal principles,
arrive at different sets of subjective preferences. There is no

10—T.P.A.

doubt that such differences will appear. Even if we assume that all rational beings accept a uniform system of *intra*personal weighting (one which balances the importance of maximizing probable benefits against the importance of minimizing maximum loss, for example)—still their preferences among interpersonal principles will differ because of differences in their circumstances, and in what they stand to gain, lose, or risk from systems governed by various principles of interpersonal combination. There is a natural conflict between a desire for maximum probable gain from the system and a desire to minimize possible loss; there is little subjective appeal in a system which will trample one underfoot for the benefit of others. If individuals consider the possibilities subjectively, these factors will influence their preference among combinatorial principles according to their assessments of their own chances.

The resulting disagreements generate a new combinatorial problem, to which no objective solution presents itself. If we can imagine that the possible principles of interpersonal combination could be enumerated and that individuals could arrive at subjective preferences among them, then if everyone ranked a certain principle first, we would have the solution. But since there is every reason to believe that this would not occur, one would have to obtain a solution through some balance among the different rankings, and the same kinds of subjective differences will arise about the best method of reaching such a balance.[1]

7. Resolution of this problem would seem to require the discovery of a subjective judgment on which everyone can agree, and whose objectification will therefore not lead to further conflict. But such agreement seems impossible to obtain under the present conditions of choice. For this reason there seems no

---

[1] It is interesting to note that if the only data available comprise a set of conflicting individual rank-*orderings* of the set of available principles of interpersonal combination, then no rational solution is possible. This follows from the Arrow Theorem, which entails that no social decision process whose data consist only of individual preference-orderings (rather than quantitative preferences) among a set of available alternatives, can satisfy simultaneously the Pareto Principle and the conditions of Collective Rationality and Non-dictatorship. See Kenneth J. Arrow, *Social Choice and Individual Values* (New York: Wiley, 2nd edn. 1963); also 'Values and Collective Decision-Making', in *Philosophy, Politics, and Society* (Third Series), ed. Peter Laslett and W. G. Runciman (Oxford: Blackwell, 1967).

alternative but to alter those conditions by placing certain
additional constraints on the subjectively determined selection
of objective principles of combination.

This may seem a peculiar step, but it can be justified in the
following way. The problem of settling on a principle of combination faces someone who *already* acknowledges the presence of
objective reasons deriving from the interests of all persons, and
who therefore must employ *some* principle for arriving at practical
conclusions on the basis of those reasons. He cannot simply do
nothing. Therefore if there appears to be no unique solution, he
must attempt to construct one by finding some measure of the
adequacy of a principle in giving full objective weight to each
individual's subjective preferences. If there is some artificially
constructed point of view from which all individuals can arrive
at subjectively determined agreement on the preferability of a
certain principle, that will provide such a measure. In fact,
there is more than one such point of view, and they yield agreement on the preferability of different principles. It is therefore
necessary to consider the methods of restriction by which these
artificial conditions of choice may be constructed, in order to
see which of them entails the least disregard for the distinctions
between those individuals whose subjective preferences are being
consulted.

The types of constraint which I shall consider all involve an
artificial imposition of uniformity on the informational conditions of choice. The inevitable difference between the preferences of individuals with a single intrapersonal weighting
system is due both to differences in taste and to differences in
their circumstances and prospects. To achieve subjective agreement we must artificially deprive each individual of the awareness of his circumstances: what he in particular has to gain or
lose from a given interpersonal weighting principle. Everyone
must choose under similar conditions of expectation. It is not
obvious that any informational restriction sufficiently strong to
produce unanimity, will not at the same time make it impossible
to give each individual's claims and needs their full weight.
However, since it seems to me the only possible line of solution,
I shall present and discuss briefly four examples of this type of
artificially constructed choice. All involve depriving the chooser
of his ordinary assumptions about who he is, and substituting

different information. All seem unsatisfactory in certain ways, but they serve to illustrate the procedure.

The first example to be considered has been mentioned already, and so has the main criticism of it. This is the utilitarian solution. It depends on an application to interpersonal conflicts of the same principles which are used to settle conflicts between reasons arising from the interests of a single person. The conditions of choice corresponding to this principle are that the chooser should treat the competing claims arising from distinct individuals as though they all arose from the interests of a single individual, himself. He is to choose on the assumption that all these lives are to be amalgamated into one life, his own. But this situation is unimaginable, and in so far as it is not, it completely distorts the nature of the competing claims, for it ignores the distinction between persons, as we have observed before.[1] To sacrifice one individual life for another, or one individual's happiness for another's is very different from sacrificing one gratification for another within a *single* life. The proposed condition of choice and the principle of combination which it supports both leave this fact out of account.

Another method of imposing unanimity, related to the first, would be to ask each person to choose a weighting system on the assumption that he is going to be assigned a role in the world at random, with an equal chance of leading the life of anyone in the population—complete with that person's preferences, tastes, and experiences.[2] If there is a rational decision function, individuals would agree about the best interpersonal weighting principle from this point of view. But although a choice under such conditions would acknowledge that the available benefits and harms were to be distributed among distinct individuals rather than being accumulated by a single individual, the decision would still depend on the conditions for weighing probable gains against probable losses for an *individual* life. In such a

---

[1] C. I. Lewis puts forward a version of the position according to which one is to imagine living the lives of all these persons *seriatim*. See *An Analysis of Knowledge and Valuation* (LaSalle, Illinois, 1946), pp. 546–7.

[2] This method has been suggested by the economist John C. Harsanyi. See 'Cardinal Utility in Welfare Economics and the Theory of Risk-Taking', *Journal of Political Economy*, LXI (October, 1953), pp. 434–5; also 'Cardinal Welfare, Individualistic Ethics, and Interpersonal Comparisons of Utility', *Journal of Political Economy*, LXIII (August, 1955), pp. 309–21.

situation it may be rational to accept a small risk of slavery or death in exchange for a very good chance of opulent luxury, if that is how the balance of social costs works out. It is tempting to feel that if one wins such a gamble, the attendant risk can be simply written off. But it is doubtful that such a feeling can provide the basis for the correct principle of interpersonal weighting, given that all of the presented lives, opulent or miserable, will be *realized*. It does not appear that the victims of such a system could admit that their claims and needs have been given due weight by it. For in the considerations which lead to the selection of that system, their lives are regarded only as possibilities; whereas in fact their sufferings are real.

The third method resembles that developed by Rawls to arrive at principles of justice for the assessment of *social institutions*.[1] It must be emphasized that he does not apply the method explicitly to the problem at hand, namely that of discovering a *general* interpersonal weighting principle to resolve conflicts between reasons and claims of whatever type. His principles are designed for the more specialized purpose of settling conflicting claims from distinct individuals or groups on the design of the common institutions of their society. Nevertheless his method, if valid, may admit of more general application than it has received in his publications so far. At any rate, it suggests a plausible method for attacking our problem, and that is what I shall discuss.

Rawls proposes that the parties to a collective choice of principles for assessing the justice of social institutions should lie under a veil of ignorance concerning their own identities and positions in society. That is the essential feature of what he calls the *original position* in which principles of assessment are to be chosen; ignorance about their own situations makes it possible for the parties to agree.

A similar original position might be utilized to produce agreement on interpersonal weighting principles of a more general nature. Each person would have to be asked to choose a principle subjectively on the assumption that his identity and position in the population are already fixed, but that he does not know who he is. What kind of choice would one make under

[1] See his article, 'Justice as Fairness' (*Philosophical Review*, 1958), reprinted in *Philosophy, Politics and Society* (Second Series) ed. Laslett and Runciman (Oxford: Blackwell, 1964).

such conditions? Rawls contends that where it is a matter of choosing principles of justice, one would reasonably choose as if one were 'designing a practice in which his enemy were to assign him his place'[1] He argues that if the choice is to determine the basic social institutions under which one must live, the factors militating for conservatism are sufficiently strong to render inappropriate a decision under the assumption that all the possibilities are equally probable. He claims that these factors require instead that one adopt a principle of overriding concern for minimization of the maximum possible loss or disadvantage under the system.

These conditions, particularly the last, seem to me difficult to establish and far from obvious. They become still less obvious if the same method is applied not to the selection of principles of social justice but to our problem of selecting a general interpersonal weighting principle. It is hard to decide how the choice of such a principle under the conditions described here will differ from a comparable choice under the conditions of the second method, described above. Moreover both methods share a common disadvantage. In the present case, as in the former one, it will be natural for the person choosing to think of the various lives, one of which he is already settled with, as *possibilities*; it is possible that he is a slave, but then again it is possible that he is a master. And he may be able to balance possibilities against each other in a way which will tolerate as an outcome of the interpersonal weighting system a small percentage of heavy losers. Such tolerance seems to deny the interests of these people due weight, since there really *are* individuals in these roles, and their lives are not possibilities, but actualities: the only lives they have. Whether or not the results of applying this method are exactly the same as those of applying the second method, both of them give rise to similar objections.

Perhaps these doubts can be answered, and if so, Rawls's method promises a solution. But I wish to suggest a fourth possibility. It is highly speculative, since I do not know how the method I am about to propose can actually be applied. Nevertheless, the conditions which it places on the choice of an interpersonal principle seem to me to grant adequate recognition to the claims of every individual being considered.

[1] Ibid., p. 139.

The proposal is this. To accord proper weight to the needs, desires, and interests of every individual, one must require that the choice of an interpersonal weighting principle be made under the condition that the chooser expects to lead *all* of the lives in question, not as a single super-life but as a set of distinct individual lives, each of them a complete set of experiences and activities. If such a decision procedure could be made intelligible, it would certainly guarantee the claims of each individual a full and equal voice in the consideration of which weighting principle to adopt—a voice not merely as a possible life but as an actual one. But it is not clear how this could be done.

I believe that the conditions of choice can be understood metaphysically, for we can imagine a person splitting into several persons, each of whom bears to the original, over time, the kind of relation that constitutes trans-temporal personal identity for an ordinary individual. Since identity of persons over time is not strict identity of person-stages, the loss of transitivity need not cause alarm. The relation between different stages of a single person is in some respects like the relation between different parts of the same thing. Two things can have some parts in common but not others, and two parts may bear the relation 'part of the same X' to a third part, without bearing that relation to each other. Similarly, two person-stages might bear the relation 'stages of the same person' to a third stage without bearing that relation to each other.

This provides a sense in which an individual might expect to become *each* of a number of different persons—not in series, but simultaneously—so that *each* of their lives would in a sense be his unique life, without deriving any compensatory or supplementary experiences, good or bad, by seepage from the other unique lives he is leading at the same time.[1]

The conditions of such a choice may therefore be imaginable. But what choice of interpersonal weighting principles would be rational under such conditions? The problem of how to adjudicate competing claims from one's various prospective selves in this hypothetical situation may be exactly the one we are trying

[1] This idea emerged during a conversation between Robert Nozick and myself, and is our joint product. Some of the relevant issues concerning personal identity are discussed by David Wiggins in *Identity and Spatio-Temporal Continuity* (Oxford: Blackwell, 1967), especially section 4.3.

to solve in terms of our model the problem of how to give due recognition to everyone's subjective preferences in a system of interpersonal combination, allowing for the fact that the reasons to be
combined stem from many individual lives and not from one mass
life with an astronomical number of experiences and episodes.

Perhaps the model is no more than an image, but it seems to
me a useful one, for it renders plausible the extremely strict
position that there can be no interpersonal compensation for
sacrifice. If one works from that position, then one will arrive
at a result similar to that which Rawls derives from his construction. That is, one will feel that first priority must be given, in
any principle of combinatorial weighting, to improving the lot
of those in the population who are worst off, and that it is
permissible to increase the benefits of those who are better off
only if it is not at a cost to those below them.[1]

Having stated the problem, and having indicated some
possible paths to its solution, I shall not attempt to pursue the
question further. It is an extremely important and difficult
question, and a substantive moral theory must try to answer it.
I am therefore not in a position to present a substantive moral
theory, but that has not been my aim. I have tried rather to
argue for certain formal conditions on rational motivation
which will determine the general form of a moral theory and
provide a partial basis for its content. It seems to me still
plausible that the solution to the problem of interpersonal combination can emerge from an application of the requirement of
objectivity. But whether or not that is so, it is important to have
shown, as I believe has been done, that the principle of objectivity does *not* automatically yield a species of utilitarianism, or
some other counter-intuitive principle, as the method for
deciding interpersonal conflicts. The requirement of objectivity
demands that full weight be accorded to the distinction between persons, and to the irreducible significance of individual
human lives, when the interests of different individuals are to be
weighed against one another in a calculus of objective reasons.
That is true even though we cannot specify the weighting system
which embodies such a respect for individuals.

[1] For a detailed exposition and defence of such a view, see Rawls's paper,
'Distributive Justice', in *Philosophy, Politics, and Society* (Third Series), ed. Laslett
and Runciman, (Oxford: Blackwell, 1967).

XIV

CONCLUSION

If the main argument of this book is correct, in what sense does it provide an answer to moral scepticism? I believe that no form of scepticism, whether epistemological or moral, can be shown to be impossible. The best one can do is to raise its cost, by showing how deep and pervasive are the disturbances of thought which it involves. There is more than one way to do this. In the present case I have tried to show that scepticism about the validity of that central class of moral reasons connected with altruism depends not just on the rejection of certain desires or sentiments, but on the abandonment of fundamental forms of practical reasoning and the conception of oneself to which they are related. The argument does not offer a justification for being moral, but it attempts to explain why typically moral justifications are capable of persuading us. And it shows that certain replies to moral arguments—denials of interest or sentiment—are inadequate because those arguments do not presuppose interest or sentiment. Their grip on us is due to something deeper.

Moral scepticism is a refusal to be persuaded by moral arguments or reasons. The object of persuasion in this case is action or desire, and that differentiates it from epistemological scepticism. The latter is a refusal to be persuaded by certain arguments or evidence, where the object of persuasion is *belief*. To defeat moral scepticism, therefore, it is not sufficient to produce the belief that certain moral statements are true, for this may leave the sceptic unpersuaded to act any differently. He may refuse to accept the fact that he *should* do something as a justification for doing or wanting to do it; i.e. he may attempt to acknowledge the truth of the statement without accepting its motivational content. It is useless to reply that he is employing the moral vocabulary incorrectly unless he uses it prescriptively, i.e. with motivational content. For if he admits that, he need only refrain from formulating moral conclusions after all, on the ground that his moral scepticism prevents him from meeting the conditions for their prescriptive employment. His scepticism is not merely a refusal to believe certain statements on their usual grounds, but a refusal to be persuaded, by considerations commonly regarded as providing moral reasons, of the justification for doing or wanting certain things. This explains why a successful attack must be directed against volitional rather than cognitive scepticism.[1]

One strategy might be to show that such scepticism conflicts radically with practical intuitions to which everyone, the sceptic included, is chronically subject and which are capable of a high degree of systematization. Such a reply may be useful if the sceptic has not been aware of the full range of judgments which his position requires him to abandon; but he may be willing to extend his doubts to the validity of all the intuitions cited.

My argument has not depended on an appeal to intuitions, except where I have tried to show that the consequences of adopting a system of objective reasons are not hopelessly at variance with intuition. Instead, I have tried to discover what the persuasiveness of moral considerations depends on, and to show that it is something whose abandonment constitutes a more radical step than a moral sceptic may have anticipated. I have tried to show that altruism and related motives do not depend on taste, sentiment, or an arbitrary and ultimate choice. They depend instead on the fact that our reasons for action are subject to the formal condition of objectivity, which depends in turn on our ability to view ourselves from both the personal and impersonal standpoints, and to engage in reasoning to practical conclusions from both of those standpoints. These are forms of thought and action which it may not be in our power to renounce. Moral scepticism therefore—the refusal to be motivationally persuaded by moral considerations—cannot be purchased at the relatively slight cost of abandoning certain sentiments or desires, or refusing to make certain choices which are in any event arbitrary. In so far as the plausibility of scepticism

---

[1] The ineffective moves described above are paralleled in epistemology by phenomenalist and conventionalist attacks on scepticism about the external world. To make claims about sensory experience logically sufficient for the truth of material object statements merely makes it impossible for the sceptic to express his doubts in 'material object' language. It does not dispel the doubts.

depends on the assumption that it involves no more than this, my argument can be regarded as a refutation.

However, that will not prevent the formation of a new scepticism at a deeper level. It is possible to ask why one should feel compelled to avoid dissociation of the two standpoints in practical matters. It is certainly conceivable that someone should be capable of arriving at motivationally effective practical judgments only from the personal standpoint; he would then be incapable of making the same judgments about others, or about himself conceived impersonally, but that involves no contradiction. If we assume that his general ability to regard the world and himself impersonally remains intact, so that he is not a total solipsist, then it will always be open to him to adopt a point of view from which all practical concerns drop away, though the circumstances under consideration remain unaltered in every detail. The same data which when viewed personally justify a practical judgment will not do so when viewed impersonally. What further objection can be raised if someone remains unabashed about coming apart in this way?

Until another argument appears which raises the cost of scepticism further by pushing the roots of moral motivation still deeper, there seems to me nothing more to be said. The fact is that although various pressures tend to cause the two standpoints to diverge in practical reasoning, and although we sustain our natural selfishness by regarding the world primarily from our own point of view, still, when the impersonal standpoint is forced upon us it becomes difficult to resist the pressures towards congruency. When they are wronged, people suddenly understand objective reasons, for they require such concepts to express their resentment. That is why the primary form of moral argument is a request to imagine oneself in the situation of another person.

Although we tend to bring the two standpoints together when a dissociation between them presents itself to us vividly, we also find many ways of avoiding such recognition, by remaining enclosed in the personal standpoint, or blotting out our sense of the reality of others. The word 'possibility' occurs in the title of this book for a reason. Even though altruistic motives depend not on love or on any other interpersonal sentiment, but on a presumably universal recognition of the reality of other persons, altruism is not remotely universal, for we continually block the effects of that recognition.

To say that altruism and morality are possible in virtue of something basic to human nature is not to say that men are basically good. Men are basically complicated; how good they are depends on whether certain conceptions and ways of thinking have achieved dominance, a dominance which is precarious in any case. The manner in which human beings have conducted themselves so far does not encourage optimism about the moral future of the species.

INDEX

Altruism, 15–17, 19, 79–84, 87–9, 127–33
Anscombe, G. E. M., 44 n.
approval, 111, 117
Aristotle, 11, 21, 29 n.
Arrow, K., 136 n.

Bad, 86 n.
Baier, K., 86
body, 75
Broad, C. D., 86 n., 96 n.
Butler, J., 81 n.

Categorical imperative, 12
competition, 131–2
conventionalism, 143–4

Desire, 4–5, 27–32; for the future, 39–46; motivated and unmotivated, 29–30, 38; natural, 74–6; unimportance, of, 128
dissociation, 58–76, 99–115, 126, 145

Edgley, R., 20 n.
egoism, 84–7, 96–7, 108, 118, 123
emotivism, 7
epistemology, 144 n.
ethical relativism, 3
externalism, 7–9

Falk, W. D., 7 n.
family commitments, 130
first person, 100–15
Frankena, W. K., 7 n.
free agent-variable, 48, 90–3
future contingencies, 54, 62 n.

Gauthier, D., 134 n.
good, 86 n.
guilt, 80 n.

Hare, R. M., 8 n.
Harman, G., vii
Harsanyi, J., 138 n.
Hobbes, 9–11, 13, 95–6
Hume, 10–13, 64
hypothetical imperative, 12

Impersonal standpoint, 100 ff.
intelligibility, 34
internalism, 7–14
interpretation, 18–19, 57–8, 99–100, 123–4, 144–5
intuition, 57, 144
intuitionism, 5

Justification, 3–4, 18, 64, 110; and explanation, 66–7, 80–1, 143

Kant, 11–14, 22

Lewis, C. I., 138 n.

Means and ends, 33–6, 51–5
Medlin, B., 86
Mill, J. S., 8
minimax, 136, 140–2
Moore, G. E., 8, 85–6
motivational content, 64 ff., 100 ff., 109 ff., 143–4
National interest, 130–1
necessity, 19–23, 123
Nietzsche, 127 n.
Nozick, R., vii, 54 n., 133 n., 141 n.

Objectivity, 82 ff.
original position, 139–40
other minds, 99–106

Patriotism, 93–5
penalties, 54
personal standpoint, 100 ff.
phenomenalism, 144 n.
Plato, 11, 58
practical reasoning, 29–30, 65, 109–10
practical solipsism, 113–15
present tense, 60–4
prudence, 15–17, 19, 36–46, 57–74
psychology, 3, 5, 19–22, 57

Quine, W. V., 22

Rawls, J., vii, 130 n., 134 n., 139–40, 142

reasons 47–56, & *passim*; combinatorial principles for, 133–4*; dated, 58 ff.; defined, 47; explanatory and normative, 15, 20–2, 57; generality of, 35; negative, 47; objective, 90 ff.; prima facie, 49–51, 66, 133; subjective, 90 ff.; timeless, 58 ff., 100; universality of, 47–8, 90, 108–9
regret, 71, 72
resentment, 83–5, 145
retribution, 46 n., 96
revenge, 46 n.
reward, 54

Scepticism, 57 n., 143–5
self-interest, 3, 16–17, 36, 48, 79–81
selfishness, 145–6

self-reliance, 92–127
social relations, 130
solipsism, 104–6
structure, 14, 31–3, 35, 80
sympathy, 80 n.

Teleology *v.* deontology, 73 n.
temporal neutrality, 61–74, 100
tenselessness, 48–9, 53 ff.
theoretical reason, 20–3, 31
time, 19, 38–46, 48, 60–71

Utilitarianism, 16, 89, 138–9, 142

Wiggins, D., vii, 143 n.
Williams, B., 71 n.
Wittgenstein, 22, 104, 106 n.